Meditation and Movement

of related interest

Mind/Body Techniques for Asperger's Syndrome
The Way of the Pathfinder
Ron Rubio
Forewords by Irene Brody and Anthony Castrogiovanni
ISBN 978 1 84310 875 7

Basic Pathfinder Mind/Body Techniques for Asperger's Syndrome (DVD)
Ron Rubio
ISBN 978 1 84310 890 0

Can't Play Won't Play
Simply Sizzling Ideas to get the Ball Rolling for Children with Dyspraxia
Sharon Drew and Elizabeth Atter
ISBN 978 1 84310 601 2

Yoga for Children with Autism Spectrum Disorders
A Step-by-Step Guide for Parents and Caregivers
Dion E. Betts and Stacey W. Betts
Forewords by Louise Goldberg, Registered Yoga Teacher and Joshua S. Betts
ISBN 978 1 84310 817 7

Writing Works
A Resource Handbook for Therapeutic Writing Workshops and Activities
Edited by Gillie Bolton, Victoria Field and Kate Thompson
ISBN 978 1 84310 468 1

Drama Therapy and Storymaking in Special Education
Paula Crimmens
ISBN 978 1 84310 291 5

Acting Antics
A Theatrical Approach to Teaching Social Understanding to Kids and Teens with Asperger Syndrome
Cindy B. Schneider
Foreword by Tony Attwood
ISBN 978 1 84310 845 0

Psychodrama
A Beginner's Guide
Zoran Djuric, Jasna Veljkovic and Miomir Tomic
ISBN 978 1 84310 411 7

Meditation and Movement

Structured Therapeutic Activity Sessions

G. Rosser

Jessica Kingsley *Publishers*
London and Philadelphia

First published in 2009
by Jessica Kingsley Publishers
116 Pentonville Road
London N1 9JB, UK
and
400 Market Street, Suite 400
Philadelphia, PA 19106, USA

www.jkp.com

Library of Congress Cataloging in Publication Data

Rosser, Garry.
Meditation and movement : structured therapeutic activity sessions / Garry Rosser.
p. cm.
Includes bibliographical references.
ISBN 978-1-84905-018-0 (pb : alk. paper) 1. Meditation--Therapeutic use. 2. Meditation for children. 3. Movement therapy for children. 4. Play therapy. I. Title.
RC489.M43R67 2009
616.89'1653--dc22

2008050200

British Library Cataloguing in Publication Data
A CIP catalogue record for this book is available from the British Library

ISBN 978 1 84905 018 0
eISBN 978 1 84642 944 6

Printed and bound in Great Britain

In memory of David Rosser
(1978–2009)

Contents

Introduction

These are sessions in meditation, writing and talking and physical activity. They are designed principally for older children and adolescents. They are for the uninitiated in meditation and for those who have little experience in therapeutic play and the martial arts.

While the sessions are conceived as an overall program, bits and pieces of them can be adapted to most school activities or used as a resource for other programs, depending on different groups' needs. For example, I have successfully run the meditation sessions separately from the movement sessions, and have used the psychodrama practices with other classroom activities. I also have used the worksheets in counselling sessions.

The length of time for each session depends on the requirements of the group and the discrimination of its leader. I have tried to pace them for about one hour each, but this is probably on the minimum side.

The overarching goal of the program is to introduce students to meditation, different therapeutic activities in different forms and to some basic skills in martial arts, and through this strengthen students' self-control, resilience and respect – both for themselves and for others.

There are four main practices that run through the sessions:

- ***a breathing technique based on a particular form of meditation.*** The form we focus on is 'Anapana sati' or 'mindfulness of breathing'

(Mindful Breathing Meditation). This form of meditation is easily accessible to older children and adolescents, as well as adults. Some relaxation exercises and visualizations are also practised in the sessions

- ***therapeutic writing and talking tasks.*** These are presented via ten worksheets found at the back of this book. Each requires group members to complete a brief reflective writing task that becomes the basis for discussion
- ***movement and psychodrama play activities.*** Sometimes called 'psychodrama' or 'play therapy' these exercises in movement explore some concerns or 'issues' common to most children and adolescents. These include friendship, trust, conflict and control
- ***breathing, posture and movement techniques found in some martial arts.*** Skills codified in the martial arts – especially in such 'soft' style martial arts as tai chi and aikido – are simplified and adapted for young people with no expertise in this field. Elementary striking, kicking and blocking techniques (for upper and lower body) are described, and disciplined engagement is encouraged.

The program is organized in three parts:

- **Sessions 1 to 5:** Each of these sessions comprises Sitting Time (elements of Mindful Breathing Meditation); Writing and Talking (tasks related to self-assessment and self-evaluation) and Movement and Games (exercises involving communication, friendship and trust). Session 5 is a review session.
- **Sessions 6 to 10:** These comprise Relaxation Exercises and Visualizations; Writing and Talking (tasks related to socialization, personal affirmation, emotional intelligence and sensory awareness) and Movement and Games (focusing on control, conflict and co-operation). Session 10 is a review session.
- **Sessions 11 to 15:** These comprise different aspects and adaptations of Mindful Breathing Meditation and breathing, postures and upper and lower body (striking, kicking and blocking) exercises in Movement. Session 15 is a review session.

Troubleshooting and **Conclusion** round off the book. These discuss some practical and theoretical considerations that arise from the program.

Not a lot of space is required to run the program. As a rule of thumb, allow enough room for each participant to make a complete turning circle with arms outstretched, without touching a neighbour. Use of space indoors or outdoors doesn't really matter. For the writing tasks a pen, paper and clipboard for all group members should be sufficient. Material that is issued to students can be photocopied from the worksheets. A few other items too are required – a stopwatch, a ball, a cushion and so on.

In developing this program I have drawn inspiration and direction from a number of key texts in the various disciplines. Most notable of these are Kamalashila's *Meditation: The Buddhist Way of Tranquility and Insight* (1992), *Group Work with Children and Adolescents: A Handbook*, edited by K.N. Dwivedi (1993), Paul Brecher's *The Way of the Spiritual Warrior* (1998) and Freerk Ykema's *Rock and Water* (c. 2000) program, which is now taught widely around the world. I acknowledge these in detail in the text.

The group's size is no less important than its age. A size of about 15 to 25 seems to work well and I advise no less than six or seven. Age-wise, 11-17-year-olds are ideal, but try to keep the group as age-homogeneous as possible. The sessions run equally well for males and females.

Before the final group is established it is a good idea to conduct pre-group interviews which clarify attendance requirements, in-house rules, any individual's particular needs or limitations, etc. Permission notes to parents/carers, too, can be issued.

There is no need for the group's leader to be a 'specialist'. Enthusiasm and reading ahead are more than enough substitute for professional 'expertise'.

Session 1

SITTING TIME[1]

Stopwatch

The session begins with the group sitting in a circle. Members try to estimate how long it takes for a minute to pass.

The leader, who has a stopwatch, controls proceedings. Group members' times can be jotted down.

If the group at first finds it too challenging to estimate a minute, it can start with half a minute and go up.

Commence with eyes open. If possible, lead to eyes closed.

This game can be played for as long as the group's interest is sustained.

What's Your Name?

Group members introduce themselves to each other. They do this first by saying their own name around the circle.

This is then repeated but now each group member adds *'and this is...'*, naming the person on their right. The group leader can be included in this.

This is repeated again, but now group members name the person on their left.

This can be extended by including the following:

- a series of objects (e.g. ball, balloon, cushion) is passed around the circle, with each passer saying the name of the receiver
- an imaginary object (e.g. fragile egg, heavy brick, tiny insect) or series of objects, is passed around the circle.

WRITING AND TALKING

Self-Assessment Quiz

This self-assessment quiz (Worksheet 1: Self-Assessment Quiz) is the basis for group members writing (completing the quiz) and talking (discussing their responses). The leader can direct this in any way felt suitable.

It involves the following, which can be discussed:

Vocabulary: honest, co-operative, reliable, popular, friendly, kind, adventurous, confident.

Concept: use of a scale (0–5).

MOVEMENT AND GAMES

Strolling

Group members stroll around the room freely, interacting with one another. Then, as determined by the group leader, strolling begins to change to varying modes. For instance, the group leader can alter the flow of the group by calling out '*stroll in slow-motion*' or '*now move quickly*' or '*smoothly*' or '*hurriedly*'.

A variation on this is when the leader directs the group to certain tasks. For instance, '*line up against the wall*', '*everybody follow this person*', '*change strolling direction*', etc.

Animal Imitation

As directed by the leader members now move in a way that imitates different animals. The leader might call out, for example, '*move with the meekness of a lamb*' or '*...the aggression of a bull*' or '*move assertively like lions*' or '*...as slippery as snakes*', etc.

Stopwatch

The session concludes with the group returning to a circle and playing Stopwatch again as they did at the session's beginning.

Session 2

SITTING TIME

Mindful Breathing[2]

Sitting in the circle, the group relaxes and attention is drawn to breathing.

The leader says:

Sit up straight, relax, rest your hands together in your lap or on your knees. Bring attention to your breathing. Keep your mouth closed. Try to keep your eyes shut but if this feels uncomfortable at the moment half-close them and focus on a point a metre or so directly in front of you, for instance, a spot on the floor.

Now, as you are breathing in and out, mark each out-breath with a mental count.

So...breathe in [the leader demonstrates by breathing in (through the nose)] *and out* [the leader demonstrates by breathing out (through the nose)], *and* ***after*** *you finish breathing out, count to yourself, in your mind, 'one'.*

Repeat this...breathe in [the leader demonstrates by breathing in] and out [the leader demonstrates by breathing out], *and* ***after*** *you finish your out-breath count to yourself, 'two'.*

Repeat this practice until you have counted ten breaths to yourself. Remember to count ***after*** *you finish breathing out.*

Try to let your breath flow naturally, without altering the way you usually breathe.

If your attention wanders, calmly bring it back to your breath and your counting.

The group does this (counting in lots of ten) for perhaps ten minutes.

WRITING AND TALKING

My Feelings, When...

Use Worksheet 2: My Feelings, When... This task personalizes and contextualizes feelings. Discussion can focus on individuals and their contexts.

MOVEMENT AND GAMES

Who's Your Partner?

The group sits in a circle, as they did in the last session, and they (re-) introduce themselves to each other by saying their own name around the circle.

Then they face the person next to them to form partners. (If there's an odd number of group members the leader can form a partnership.) The aim of the task is for each member to discover three pieces of information about their partner. They'll need to do this by talking and asking questions.

Facing the circle each member introduces their partner to the group and says three things about them to the whole group.

Things said must be positive; no put-downs.

An extension of this – which can be used depending on the group's confidence – is that each member again (re-)introduces themselves to the group by saying their own name, now adding one thing (building up to three things) that they *like* about themselves. This can be done by saying something like: *'Hi. My name is...and something(s) I like is/are...'*.

They then talk to, and ask questions of, their partner, and facing the circle each member (re-)introduces their partner to the group and says one thing (building up to three things) that they *like* about their partner. This can be done by saying something like: *'Hi. This is...and something(s) I like about them is/are...'*.

Again, negatives and put-downs are prohibited.

Session 3

SITTING TIME

Mindful Breathing

Sitting in a circle the group, under the leader's direction, reviews and practises the form of breathing learned in the last session. This goes on for perhaps five minutes.

The leader says:

While you are doing this form of meditation begin to bring your attention to the point on your face where you feel the air making contact. This will be in or around your nostrils and upper lip. Let your attention rest there. Try to stay focused on this point.

In other words, when you breathe in and out try to bring your attention to the flow of air at your nostrils – while still counting to yourself after you have finished your out-breath. The air at your nostrils may feel cool as it enters and warm as it leaves. Be receptive to it, observing the experience without becoming attached or engaged in it.

So...breathe in, focusing your mind on the flow of air at your nostrils [the leader demonstrates by breathing in], *and out, still focusing your mind on the flow of air at your nostrils* [the leader demonstrates by breathing out], *and after you finish breathing out, count to yourself, in your mind, 'one'.*

Then you repeat this...breathe in, and out, paying attention to the air at your nostrils, and after you finish your out-breath count to yourself, 'two'.

Repeat this until you have counted ten breaths to yourself. Remember to try to stay focused on the airflow at your face, as well as to count after you finish breathing out.

The group does this (counting in lots of ten) for perhaps ten minutes.

WRITING AND TALKING

Mood Quiz

Use Worksheet 3: Mood Quiz. This mood scale is the basis for group members writing (completing the scale) and talking (discussing their responses). It is conducted under the leader's supervision.

The following can be discussed:

Vocabulary: happy, worried, bad-tempered, liked, different, depressed, frightened, positive.

Concept: use of a scale (0–10).

MOVEMENT AND GAMES

Review

Begin this part of this session by reviewing any of the first two sessions' movement activities. Run through again whatever feels suitable.

Rocking in a Circle

For this exercise the group stands in a fairly tight circle facing inwards. A volunteer goes to the middle and stands with their feet together, their body quite rigid and their arms by their sides.

Those in the circle now stretch out their arms towards the volunteer, gently holding them with their hands.

The volunteer then leans backwards, then forwards and so on, supported by the outstretched arms of those in the circle who gently rock them in different directions.

Different volunteers might like to experience being supported and rocked in this way.

Rocking with Partners

This is an activity with partners. If group members are undecided regarding who to choose as partners, the same partnerships from the last session can be re-formed.

One partner stands in front of the other, with their feet together, their body quite rigid and their arms by their sides. The other stretches out their arms and gently holds the partner by the shoulders.

The first partner then leans backwards, then forwards and so on, supported by the outstretched arms of the other who rocks them gently.

Roles are then reversed.

'Magic Shop' Game[3]

This game involves a lot of talking. Group members 'trade' or 'swap' some of their personal qualities with other members. For example, if a group member has a lot of one quality (e.g. being 'cool') this can be swapped (with another member) for a quality he or she is lacking (e.g. being 'over-sensitive'). The 'magic shop' thus serves as a forum for individuals to identify and discuss their strengths and weaknesses.

It is important that participants feel safe from embarrassment or humiliation as a consequence of disclosing their feelings.

Having completed this, group members can then 'act out' their newly gained (and lost) qualities through directly addressing the group (verbally) in their new personas or in strolling around freely, portraying their newly acquired attributes (as gestures, postures and poses).

Session 4

SITTING TIME

Mindful Breathing

Under the leader's direction the group reviews and practises the form of meditation learned in the second session. This goes on for perhaps five minutes.

The leader says:

We are now going to alter this form of meditation slightly by counting to ourselves ***before****, rather than after, each breath. You still keep your attention at your nostrils and upper lip, but* ***before*** *you breathe in and out try to mark each in-breath with a mental count. You will notice a qualitative change in the feeling of the meditation.*

*So...****before*** *you breathe in count 'one', and focusing your mind on the flow of air at your nostrils, breathe in* [the leader demonstrates by breathing in], and then out [the leader demonstrates by breathing out], *all the time focusing your mind on the flow of air at your nostrils.*

Then you repeat this... You count 'two' to yourself ***before*** *breathing in, then out, all the time paying attention to the air at your nostrils.*

Repeat this until you have counted ten breaths to yourself. Remember to try to stay focused on the airflow at your face, as well as to count ***before*** *you start your in-breath.*

The group does this (counting in lots of ten) for perhaps ten minutes.

WRITING AND TALKING

Mood Quiz (revisited)

The Mood Quiz introduced in the last session is revisited. Today the group undertakes the writing task (completing the scale) again. They discuss their responses this week to last week's responses, comparing differences.

Mood Quiz Vocabulary

There are two lists of words: Worksheet 4A for younger (Juniors) and Worksheet 4B for older (Seniors) group members. Individuals select two or three (or more) words that best describe their current state of mind. This becomes the basis of a discussion.

MOVEMENT AND GAMES

Pushing–Pulling

In pairs, partners sit on the floor facing each other, soles of feet pushing against each other. Arms outstretched, they grasp hands and gently push and pull each other, rocking backward and forward.

Mirroring

Again, sitting on the floor facing each other, one partner imitates the movement of the other (e.g. raising an arm), acting as the partner's 'mirror'. Roles are then reversed.

Pushing Up

Maintaining their pairs, partners sit on the floor back to back. Pushing against each other's back, they lock arms with each other and try to stand up, pushing with only their backs for support. This is quite a physically challenging exercise.

'Survival' Game

This game is sometimes called 'Lifeboat'. In it the group pretends to have gathered together either in an imaginary nuclear shelter (to stay until it is safe to go outside) or in a lifeboat (after their ship has sunk). Unfortunately, in order for the rest of the group to survive (e.g. because of a food shortage) one of the group members has to leave the shelter/lifeboat. The group as a whole must decide who will leave and who will stay.

Before commencing the game, assign roles to group members: e.g.:

- ten-year-old school child – male or female; describe personality; other features, etc.
- teenager – male or female; describe personality, etc.
- working adult – male or female; nominate age, personality, features, etc.
- retired scientist – male or female; this person may have a 'solution' to problem, etc.
- young mother with baby – nominate particular characteristics, etc.

Session 5: Review

SITTING TIME

Mindful Breathing

This session reviews all three stages of meditation practice outlined in previous sessions.

Sitting in a circle, under the leader's direction, the group relaxes and draws attention to breathing.

First, the leader says:

Sit up straight, relax, rest your hands together in your lap or on your knees. Bring attention to your breathing.

As you are breathing in and out, mark each out-breath with a mental count.

So...breathe in [the leader demonstrates by breathing in (through the nose)] *and out* [the leader demonstrates by breathing out (through the nose)], *and* ***after*** *you finish breathing out, count to yourself, in your mind, 'one'.*

Repeat this...breathe in [the leader demonstrates by breathing in] *and out* [the leader demonstrates by breathing out], *and* ***after*** *you finish your out-breath count to yourself, in your mind, 'two'.*

Repeat this practice until you have counted ten breaths to yourself. Remember to count ***after*** *you finish breathing out.*

Try to let your breath flow naturally, without altering the way you usually breathe.

If your attention wanders, calmly bring it back to your breath and your counting.

Then, the leader says:

While you are doing this form of meditation begin to bring your attention to the point on your face where you feel the air making contact. This will be in or around your nostrils and upper lip. Let your attention rest there. Try to stay focused on this point.

*In other words, when you breathe in and out try to bring your attention to the flow of air at your nostrils – while still counting to yourself **after** you have finished your out-breath. The air at your nostrils may feel cool as it enters and warm as it leaves. Be receptive to it, observing the experience without becoming attached or engaged in it.*

So...breathe in, focusing your mind on the flow of air at your nostrils [the leader demonstrates by breathing in], *and out, still focusing your mind on the flow of air at your nostrils* [the leader demonstrates by breathing out], *and **after** you finish breathing out, count to yourself, in your mind, 'one'.*

*Then you repeat this...breathe in, and out, paying attention to the air at your nostrils, and **after** you finish your out-breath you count to yourself, in your mind, 'two'.*

*Repeat this until you have counted ten breaths to yourself. Remember to try to stay focused on the airflow at your face, as well as to count **after** you finish breathing out.*

The group does this (counting in lots of ten) for perhaps five minutes.

Next, the leader says:

We are now going to alter this form of meditation slightly by counting to ourselves ***before****, rather than after, each breath. You still keep your attention at your nostrils and upper lip, but* ***before*** *you breathe in and out try to mark each in-breath with a mental count. You will notice a qualitative change in the feeling of the meditation.*

*So...***before** *you breathe in count 'one', and focusing your mind on the flow of air at your nostrils, breathe in* [the leader demonstrates by breathing in]*, and then out* [the leader demonstrates by breathing out]*, all the time focusing your mind on the flow of air at your nostrils.*

Then you repeat this... You count 'two' to yourself ***before*** *breathing in, then out, all the time paying attention to the air at your nostrils.*

Repeat this until you have counted ten breaths to yourself. Remember to try to stay focused on the airflow at your face, as well as to count ***before*** *you start your in-breath.*

The group does this (counting in lots of ten) for perhaps ten minutes.

Finally, the leader says:

Relax for a moment or two.

Now, this time we are going to stop counting altogether. Be sure to maintain attention at your nostrils and upper lip. In other words, when you breathe in and out try to bring your attention to the flow of air at your nostrils without thinking any more about counting.

The air at your nostrils may feel cool as it enters and warm as it leaves. Be receptive to it, observing the experience without becoming attached or engaged in it.

So...breathe in, focusing your mind on the flow of air at your nostrils [the leader demonstrates by breathing in]*, and out, still focusing your mind on the flow of air at your nostrils* [the leader demonstrates by breathing out].

Keep practising this form of mindful breathing. This is the form of meditation we have been striving for.

The group does this for perhaps ten minutes.

WRITING AND TALKING

Review

In this session the group can revisit any of the earlier sessions' Writing and Talking tasks. Run through again whatever feels suitable.

The tasks are:

- Self-Assessment Quiz
- My Feelings, When…
- Mood Quiz
- Mood Quiz Vocabulary (Juniors/Seniors).

MOVEMENT AND GAMES

Eyes Open–Eyes Closed

In pairs, a partner (eyes open) leads their friend (eyes closed) around the room, carefully telling them where they are going and quietly and supportively introducing them to other pairs.

This game can be extended by adding another friend (eyes closed) to the pair, making a longer and longer human chain.

Knotted

The group divides into two teams.

One team leaves the room for a moment while the remaining team members stand in a circle holding hands. They then tangle themselves into a 'knot', by stepping over linked arms, crawling between legs, etc. – all the time holding hands.

The team from outside the room is then invited to work out a way to 'untie' the 'knot' without disconnecting the hands.

The teams then reverse roles.

Review

Revisit any of the movement activities from the earlier sessions:

- Strolling
- Animal Imitation
- Stopwatch
- Who's Your Partner?
- Rocking in a Circle
- Rocking with Partners
- 'Magic Shop' Game
- Pushing–Pulling
- Mirroring
- Pushing Up
- 'Survival' Game.

Session 6

RELAXATION EXERCISES

Lying Down (I)

Strictly speaking, meditation is not 'relaxation'. Meditation involves harmonizing energy, attention and focus, while relaxation tends to dissipate energy throughout the body. In relaxation the mind is 'slowed down' through the participant's willingness to focus upon his or her body, often setting aside consciousness to thoughts and emotions. In this way body calmness and rejuvenation are achieved. Relaxation exercises are often used to counter stress.

The following exercises should therefore be approached as tools to calm the mind and body, restore energy and instil in the meditator a sense of self-control and empowerment. If, however, group members feel frustrated at the lack of mental direction, they can practise Mindful Breathing Meditation. That is, while they are following the leader's relaxation instructions they can maintain mindfulness of their breathing, focusing on the flow of air at the nostrils.

The leader says:

Find a comfortable space on the floor, lie on your back, stretch out, let your arms and body and legs rest completely easily. Close your eyes.

We are going to become totally relaxed, letting our energy dissipate throughout our body and our mind calm down. If however, during the following you start to feel frustrated at the lack of mental direction, you can practise the Mindful Breathing Meditation we have learned so far. In other words, follow my [the leader's] *directions in the Relaxation Exercises but, if you choose, simultaneously keep mindful of your breathing, focusing on the flow of air at the nostrils.*

Let's begin by keeping very still, and focusing on our breath, breathe in...and out..., in...and out..., until your breath is regular and comfortable.

Notice that your body is in contact with the floor.

Bring your concentration to the point of contact between the back of your head and the floor, between your arms and the floor, and now between your shoulders and the floor.

Bring your concentration to the point of contact between your hips and the floor, your buttocks and the floor, your thighs and the floor, your calves and the floor, and now your heels and the floor.

Notice all these points of contact very carefully. Go over them again, one by one, until you can experience these points like one single plane of contact between your whole body and the floor.

While you are in this state of relaxation image you are in a place that is totally safe for you. It is a place where you are safe and protected from anything that might hurt or bother you. In this place you are totally secure.

In your imagination, look around. Notice things that are close to you. Notice their colours and smells and their textures. Notice any sounds. Notice exactly what they are. In your imagination you can pick objects up and examine them or just notice them casually. These are things that make you happy. These are things that don't judge you. These are things that make you feel good about yourself.

Now notice things that are further away. They are a little way off in the distance. You can walk towards them if you want or just look at them from where you are. Again you can notice them in detail – what their colours are, what sounds they make, what smells they carry, their textures and so on.

Now, when you are ready, return to the things that are close by you in your imagination.

For a moment look closely at them again, then prepare yourself to leave them and to come back into your body.

Notice your whole body again. Experience it as if it is floating on the surface of the floor. Bring your concentration to the point of contact between your heels and the floor, feeling this point as light and full of energy. Now bring your concentration to your calves, and thighs, and buttocks, feeling each point as light and energized.

Now pay attention to the point of contact between your hips and the floor, your shoulders, your arms and finally the back of your head and the floor, experiencing each point as light and strong.

Experience your whole body as light and energized, powerful, strong and refreshed.

When you are completely ready slowly open your eyes. Lie quietly for a moment. You might want or to yawn or stretch before getting up. Slowly get to your feet and rejoin the group.

At this point the group might like to discuss what their experience was like, and whether they feel calmer, energized and more powerful.

WRITING AND TALKING

Friendship Quiz

Use Worksheet 5: Friendship Quiz. This rating scale is the basis for group members writing (completing the scale) and talking (discussing their responses).

Vocabulary: listen properly, respect, attitudes, beliefs, views, feelings, motivate, support, cope.

Making a Sociogram

Use Worksheet 6: Making a Sociogram. This task requires group members to make a sociogram, mapping their friendship circle(s). The key feature of a sociogram is that it shows how individuals are connected, either directly or indirectly.

Group members' sociograms form the basis of discussion.

MOVEMENT AND GAMES

Who's Your Partner? (revisited)

The group sits in a circle; each person introduces themselves, and says one thing (building up to three things) that they like about themselves.

They then talk and ask questions of their partner, and facing the circle each member introduces their partner to the group and says one thing (building up to three things) that they like about their partner.

Sculpting in Pairs

With this partner, they then form pairs, and stand facing each other.

One partner then moves ('sculpts') the body and limbs of the other into a (comfortable) position by physically moving the partner's body into a pose that 'freezes'.

The 'sculpted' partner holds this 'frozen' position and is 'photographed' by their partner with an imaginary camera.

Roles are then reversed.

Sculpting the Group

A volunteer member of the group 'sculpts' the rest of the group (or a group of 'friends') in a (comfortable) group pose.

All 'sculpted' group members hold their 'frozen' positions until they have been 'photographed' by the 'sculptor'.

New volunteers are then called for.

Each group member has a turn at 'sculpting'.

Guess Who?

This game involves participants strolling about silently with cards stuck on their foreheads (use double-sided tape). Every card has one duplicate copy (there are two lots of the same card).

Each participant has a different card and doesn't know what is written on it. They only know what is written on others' cards (not their own).

These cards have been prepared beforehand and contain messages that have been offered by the group: such as 'I talk too much; please make me listen'; 'I am lonely; help me find a friend' and 'As we talk, please mirror my posture, gestures and expressions'.

The aim of the game is to find the person who has the same card as yours. You then share (verbally) the feelings aroused by the responses you have received.

Session 7

RELAXATION EXERCISES

Lying Down (2)

Like the previous relaxation exercise this one also can be used to counter stress and instil personal strength. Again, too, if group members choose they can practise Mindful Breathing Meditation while following the leader's instructions.

The leader says:

Find a comfortable space on the floor, lie on your back, stretch out, letting your arms and body and legs rest completely easily. Close your eyes.

Let your body relax, still your mind and focus your breath, breathing in…and out…, in…and out…, until your breath is regular and comfortable. If you choose, you can practise Mindful Breathing Meditation while following my [the leader's] *directions in this Relaxation Exercise.*

Lie completely still.

Bring your awareness to the muscles in your face and head. For a moment, try to tighten the muscles in your head…then relax them. Feel the muscles in your jaw, tighten them for a moment…then relax them. Think of your face and your forehead and your eyes. Tighten all the muscles here, just for a moment. Hold them tight… then relax them. Let your face become soft and smooth and your head very still and heavy and relaxed.

Think of your whole right arm, and just for a moment tighten all the muscles here, in that arm. Now release the tension. Think of your left arm. For a moment tighten the muscles here, hold them tightly for a moment…then release them. Both arms are now released and free. They feel loose and warm and heavy.

Move your awareness to your whole right leg, and for a moment tighten all the muscles in this leg…then let the tension go. Move your awareness to your left leg and do the same. Tighten the muscles here for a moment…then release them. Now both legs should be feeling released and free from tension.

Move your awareness to the muscles in your back and shoulders. Stretch out and tighten the muscles here. Hold them tight for a moment, then when you are ready… release them. Your back and shoulders should feel loose and relaxed.

Feel your whole body's relaxation. You are feeling calm and peaceful.

Imagine yourself in a beautiful peaceful place. It is somewhere where you feel safe and happy. Somewhere without stress or anxiety, judgement or fear, trouble or annoyance. You can be yourself here, in this peaceful place.

See yourself in this place. You are calm, happy, very relaxed and at peace. Stay here for a while enjoying your peaceful place in silence...

When you are ready, slowly leave that peaceful place and think again of the room you are in. Think of your face and head...; your whole right arm...; your left arm...; your whole right leg...; then your left leg...; and finally think of your back and shoulders.

Your whole body now feels calm and refreshed. When you are ready slowly open your eyes, stretch, get up and rejoin the group.

WRITING AND TALKING

Affirmations

Use Worksheet 7: Affirmations. This reflective task is based on the group writing (briefly) in the balloons and talking about their written responses.

Thoughts and Feelings

Use Worksheet 8: Thoughts and Feelings. This task follows the one immediately above. Group members write three thoughts that make them feel good about themselves and three thoughts that make them feel bad. They then write down three feelings they like and dislike. These lists are the basis for discussion.

MOVEMENT AND GAMES

Breaking in–Breaking out

The group stands in a circle with tightly linked arms and a volunteer goes first into the middle of the circle, then outside the circle. The game involves the volunteer attempting to break out or enter into the circle while the group tries to prevent this from happening.

Different volunteers take turns at breaking in and/or out of the circle.

ABC

A variation of this game is often played in theatre sports.[4]

The group sits in a circle and invents a 'story' in which each successive speaker around the circle adds a piece of dialogue that must begin with the next letter of the alphabet. The story commences with the first speaker starting a word with the letter 'A'.

For example, for the 'M, N, O, P' part of the story the dialogue could run something like:

'**M**y Mother dropped eggs all over the floor.'

'**N**ever had I seen such a mess!'

'**O**nly yesterday I'd cleaned the floor too!'

'**P**oor Mum! I did feel sorry for her, but then again sometimes she can be mean.'

The game ends when the entire alphabet has been completed.

Session 8

VISUALIZATIONS

Lying Down (3)

While relaxation exercises principally disperse energy throughout the body, in Visualizations (sometimes called Guided Meditations) the participant's imagination comes to the fore to evoke calmness, strength and nourishment. Visualizations are different from other forms of meditation in that they alert the mind to inner narratives, pulling together thoughts and emotions, but setting aside consciousness of this same mental activity. Visualizations are often used to refocus direction. Like relaxation they are often used to counter stress.

Again, if group members feel frustrated at the lack of direction, they can practise Mindful Breathing Meditation while still engaging in this part of the session.

The leader says:

Find a comfortable space on the floor, lie on your back, stretch out, let your arms and body and legs rest completely easily. Close your eyes.

Now we are going to become totally relaxed, letting our energy disperse throughout our body and our mind wander. Again though, if you want, during the following visualization you can bring your attention to the flow of air at the nostrils. Let's begin...

Lie completely still.

Lying like this and keeping your eyes closed, visualize walking into a wide meadow on a warm breezy summer day. In your mind, see yourself standing still, looking around. Notice some flowers blowing in the wind, bending back and forth in a regular rhythm, over and over again, just as your breath is coming in and flowing out regularly and evenly.

Enjoy the relaxed feeling in your body while watching the wind gently blow the flowers back and forth. Let yourself feel whole and comfortable in your resting body.

Now, after some time, and when you are completely ready, leave the meadow and walk towards the ocean nearby. The sun is bright, the sky is clear and the water is before you. You feel sand beneath your feet and between your toes. The sun warms your body and a gentle breeze brushes against your face.

For a moment you are standing still, looking around, watching the waves wash against the shoreline in their regular rhythms, over and over again. Watching the regular pattern of the waves you breathe in and out, evenly in and out, over and over.

Enjoy the relaxed feeling in your body.

Now, when enough time has passed and you are ready, begin to come back to your everyday active self. Move your toes, then your fingers, then your legs and arms as you shift from your imagination back to the real world around you. Stretch out your legs and arms and arch your back. Take one or two very deep breaths. Slowly open your eyes. Sit up, then rejoin the group.

WRITING AND TALKING

What Are Your Preferred Senses?

Use Worksheet 9: What Are Your Preferred Senses? This task allows the group to explore different sensory preferences – visual, aural or kinaesthetic. Their preferred sense is most likely to be their dominant learning sense.

This is both an informative and reflective task.

MOVEMENT AND GAMES

Pushing Up (revisited)

This exercise was undertaken in an earlier session. It is repeated now.

In pairs, partners sit on the floor back to back. Pushing against each other's backs, they lock arms with each other and try to stand up, pushing with only their backs for support. This is quite a physically challenging exercise.

Pushing Up in a Circle

This is a group variation on Pushing Up.

All group members sit on the floor in a circle, facing outwards. They lock arms with their neighbour on left and right and the whole group tries to stand up. They have only their own strength (in their legs) and their neighbours' shoulders for support.

Freeze–Thaw

Like ABC (in Session 7, above) a variation of this game is sometimes played in theatre sports where it is known as Space Jumps.

The group sits in a (large) circle with two members in the middle. These two play the role of actors who begin a scene of their choice.

At any time a group member from the circle can shout '*Freeze*', which 'freezes' the scene. This circle member then gets up and replaces one of the two 'actors'. The new 'actor' shouts '*Thaw*' and the scene resumes.

A twist in this game is that when '*Thaw*' is shouted the new scene takes place some time previously. For example:

> A school principal is discussing an 'incident' that has happened at school with a student. The student is pleading his 'innocence'.
>
> FREEZE: (The new actor replaces the student. The actor plays the role of a teacher.)
>
> THAW: The teacher explains to the principal that the student is not so 'innocent' at all. In fact, the student was seen being insensitive and provocative to someone else.
>
> FREEZE: (The new actor replaces the principal. The actor plays the role of the student's parent.)
>
> THAW: The parent explains to the teacher that there has been an ongoing issue at school involving quite a few students. This particular student has been unfairly singled out.
>
> Etc.

Session 9

GUIDED MEDITATION: LOVING KINDNESS

Thoughts and Feelings Meditation

'Loving kindness meditation' guides our thoughts and feelings towards friendliness, concern and kindness towards ourselves and others. This not only makes us feel better but, according to Buddhism, combats negative feelings in the world. This meditation is structured as three 10–15-minute meditations commencing with ourselves, then moving to someone in particular we love and concluding with everyone in general. If you wish to stop at any point during the meditations, do so. You can always return later.

Loving kindness towards yourself

The leader says:

Sit up straight, relax, rest your hands together in your lap or on your knees. Keep your mouth closed. Keep your eyes shut.

Bring your focus to your mind. Try to focus away from your body – away from how you are sitting, away from your breathing, and so on – and concentrate just on your thoughts and feelings as they come and go in your mind. When your mind is peaceful you can be attentive to your thoughts and emotions.

When you are ready ask yourself: 'How are you? How are you really at the moment – this exact moment in your life?' And when you ask yourself this try to be aware of your immediate, impulsive response to this question. Don't try to articulate or intellectualize or judge it, just experience this response, whatever it is. Sit with it for a moment or two and acknowledge that this is how you are thinking and feeling right here, now.

Then, no matter whatever your response, wish yourself happiness, love and kindness. You might say to yourself, for example: 'May I be well and happy' or 'I am a good and wise person' or 'I am loving and strong', or any similar short affirmation. Choose a positive phrase like this and say it to yourself a number of times. Try to feel the meaning of the words. Really try to believe what you are saying. Try for a moment to focus powerfully upon yourself in as kind and forgiving and loving way as you can. Hold the phrase you have chosen the way you'd hold something that is fragile and precious in the palm of your hand. Dwell on it. Think about it.

When distractions arise acknowledge them, then let them pass. Return again and again to your self-affirmation.

When you are ready you can conclude this part of your loving kindness meditation by saying to yourself:

May I be safe from danger;

May I be happy;

May I be healthy and strong and clear;

May wellbeing be mine.

Loving kindness towards someone we love

Continue to sit quietly, mouth closed, eyes shut, focusing upon your thoughts and feelings.

Bring to mind someone who is close to you, someone you love and care for and respect – a friend is a good idea. But avoid someone about whom you have sexual feelings – this will complicate your meditation and you'll get confused. You may have an image of this person in your mind or you may picture a scene that involves them or you may just have a strong general sense of them.

Really concentrate on this person you love. You might say to them in your mind, for example: 'May you be well and happy' or 'You are a loving person' or 'You are good and wise and strong', or any similar phrase that affirms them. Repeat this a number of times until you can really feel the meaning of the words. Focus powerfully upon the person in as kind and loving a way as you can.

Now notice how you are responding to your projected loving kindness. Notice that even though you may love this person as a close friend, you may still be holding back some feelings about them. Try to be as emotionally honest as you can. You don't have to do anything – just note what you are feeling.

If you do have some difficulty with this, stay with it. You may well learn something new about yourself. Don't forget this is your meditation. It is about you as much as anyone else. You are in control. You are making the choices.

During this process when distractions arise acknowledge them, then let them pass, and return to your affirmation.

You might conclude by saying to yourself about the person:

May you be happy and peaceful;

May you enjoy strength, vitality and good health;

May wellbeing be yours.

Loving kindness towards everyone

Start this meditation by thinking of the four people you've considered in the earlier stages – yourself, someone you love, someone who is neutral in your life at the moment and someone you find challenging. Try to picture them all together. Now send each of them equally a feeling of concern and goodwill. Don't try to compare them to each other. Concentrate on your own feeling. It is the same feeling you are sending yourself and your companions.

Now bring your thoughts back to yourself. As you did in the Loving kindness towards yourself meditation give yourself your own loving kindness. Say to yourself:

May I be safe from danger;

May I be happy;

May I be healthy and strong and clear;

May wellbeing be mine.

Then, when you are ready, extend that feeling to anyone who is around you – next to you, in the room, in the house or in the building where you're meditating. Try to keep this feeling strong. Focus on the feeling as clearly as you can and send it out from you.

Now extend it beyond the house or building to your neighbourhood. You might want to say in your mind, for example: 'May you all be well and happy' or 'May you all be good and wise and strong' or 'May you all be loving', or any similar affirmative phrase. Repeat this a number of times until you can really feel strongly the meaning of the words.

Finally, extend your loving kindness across the country and throughout the world. Stay with this feeling until you are ready to conclude. End the whole session by saying to yourself:

May everyone be happy;

May everyone be peaceful;

May everyone enjoy strength and good health;

May everyone enjoy wellbeing.

WRITING AND TALKING

Affirmations (Revisited)

This reflective task was undertaken in an earlier session. It is repeated now with two added variations. Use Worksheet 7: Affirmations. Once group members have written (briefly) in the balloons about themselves, they write about someone in particular they love (changing the inner box to 'What you are good at') and everyone in general, making affirmations about all people (changing the inner box to 'What we are good at').

Finally, group members talk about all their written responses.

MOVEMENT AND GAMES

Strengths and Challenges

Sitting in a circle, members first introduce themselves by saying their name, then they say something about themselves that they believe to be a strength (or something that they like about themselves), then something about themselves that they believe to be a challenge (or something that they don't like about themselves).

This is then repeated but now each group member introduces the person on their right, saying something about this person that they find a strength, then something about this person that they find a challenge.

This is repeated again, but now group members introduce the person on their left with the 'strength' and 'challenge' call.

This can be extended by introducing people in the group who are directly opposite, or people with whom strong eye contact is made, or people with whom no eye contact is made, etc.

This can be a difficult exercise for some people. It is important at the end that everyone feels included and affirmed. To conclude, therefore, the group leader sums up the positive attributes for each participant and the positive attributes of the group as a whole.

Open Story

Like ABC and Freeze – Thaw (in Sessions 7 and 8, above) Open Story has its origins in theatre sports.

The core game comprises group members sitting in a (large) circle and a volunteer offering to commence telling a story. They speak for about a minute, improvising as they go. When a 'paragraph' or so is told the next person in the circle takes over, continuing to embellish or alter the content. The story is completed around the circle.

There are many variations to this. One is that group members may prefer to 'act' their part of the story. They do this by moving into the centre of the circle and 'acting out' or miming their contribution. Another is that the group leader nominates participants who must be next in the story-telling, as either 'speakers' or 'actors'. Still another is that each participant contributes only a single word (or action) to the story, – this must be without hesitation or repetition. Participants are counted 'out' of the story-telling if they fail to do this. The 'winner' is left to complete the story any way they like.

Session 10: Review

RELAXATION AND VISUALIZATION WITH MUSIC

Relaxation and visualization can be practised with music – without a voice-over instructing or guiding the participant. Listening to appropriate music (or natural sounds) can quieten the mind and slow the heart rate. This in turn lowers stress levels and enhances feelings of calm and wellbeing.

There is an abundance of 'relaxation' and 'stress management' music, and recordings of natural sounds on the market.[5]

The leader says:

Find a comfortable space on the floor, lie on your back, stretch out, letting your arms and body and legs rest completely easily. Close your eyes.

Today we are going to do another form of relaxation and visualization, guided not by a spoken commentary but by recorded music and natural sounds. Let your thoughts flow according to the music. While you are listening, try to be mindful of your breathing, focusing on the flow of air at the nostrils.

Lie completely still. Relax. Try to watch your mind drift according to what you are hearing.

WRITING AND TALKING

Review

In this session the group can revisit any of the earlier sessions' Writing and Talking tasks. Run through again whatever feels suitable.

The more recent tasks are:

- Friendship Quiz
- Making a Sociogram
- Affirmations
- Thoughts and Feelings
- What Are Your Preferred Senses?

MOVEMENT AND GAMES

Eyes Open–Eyes Closed

In pairs, a partner (eyes open) leads their friend (eyes closed) around the room, carefully telling them where they are going and quietly and supportively introducing them to other pairs.

This game can be extended by adding another friend (eyes closed) to the pair, making a longer and longer human chain.

Knotted

The group divides into two teams. One team leaves the room for a moment while the remaining team members stand in a circle holding hands.

They then tangle themselves into a 'knot', by stepping over linked arms, crawling between legs, etc. – all the time holding hands.

The team from outside the room is then invited to work out a way to 'untie' the 'knot' without disconnecting the hands.

The teams then reverse roles.

Review

The group can revisit any of the favoured movement activities from earlier sessions.

These are:

- Sculpting in Pairs
- Sculpting the Group
- Guess Who?
- Breaking In–Breaking Out
- ABC
- Pushing Up In A Circle
- Freeze–Thaw
- Strengths and Challenges
- Open Story.

Session 11

MINDFUL BREATHING MEDITATION

This session reviews the meditation practice learned in earlier sessions of the program. It is important to do the following in the order suggested.

The group leader says:

We are going to review what we've learned already.

Sit cross-legged, back held straight, and face forward. Rest your hands in your lap. Close your eyes.

Breathe evenly in and out.

As you are breathing in and out, mark each out-breath with a mental count ***after*** *you finish breathing out. Do this while maintaining your mind's focus on the flow of air at your nostrils. So...breathe in* [the leader demonstrates] *and out* [the leader demonstrates] *and* ***after*** *you finish your out-breath count to yourself, 'one'. Do the same for 'two', and so on until you have counted ten breaths to yourself. Remember to count* ***after*** *you finish breathing out and stay focused on the airflow at your face.*

The group does this (counting in lots of ten) for perhaps five minutes.

Then the leader says:

Relax for a moment or two.

Now we are going to alter this form of meditation slightly by counting to ourselves ***before****, rather than after, each breath. Again, do this while maintaining focus on the flow of air at your nostrils. So...* ***before*** *you breathe in count 'one'* [the leader demonstrates] *and then out* [the leader demonstrates]. *Repeat this, counting 'two', and so on until you have counted ten breaths to yourself. Remember to count* ***before*** *you breathe in and stay focused on the airflow at your face.*

The group does this (counting in lots of ten) for perhaps five minutes.

Then the leader says:

Relax for a moment or two.

Now, stop counting altogether but maintain attention at your nostrils and upper lip. In other words, when you breathe in and out try to bring your attention to the flow of air at your nostrils without thinking any more about counting.

The group does this for perhaps ten minutes.

This is the form of mindful breathing meditation we have been aiming to achieve.

MOVEMENT: GROUNDED[6]

Feeling Grounded

The group stands either in a circle facing inwards, or as individuals scattered in a room, facing the same direction.

The leader says:

Stand comfortably balanced, feet shoulder-width apart, knees slightly bent.

Now instead of breathing in and out through the nose as we do for meditation, we are going to breathe in through our nose and out through our mouth. We breathe in through our nose because this warms the air as it enters our breathing passages, and we breathe out through our mouth so that the air can escape with maximum speed.

Experience yourself as though you are firmly grounded to the floor. First, try to grip the surface with your toes, wriggling them and moving energy into your feet and legs. Keep your back straight and your knees bent. Let your arms hang loosely by your sides.

Now visualize your feet stuck into the floor. Imagine them big and strong and powerful.

Feel the energy in the lower part of your body and try to locate, mentally, your body's centre of gravity. This is towards your abdomen, below and behind your navel. Mentally picture your body growing from the floor, standing strong and powerful.

For a moment or two rock slightly on your feet. Experience the feeling of being 'grounded' to the floor.

This is your 'grounded' position.

Leg Swinging

The leader says:

Now, when you are completely balanced, shift your weight slightly to one leg and commence swinging the other. (It doesn't matter which leg you start with.) Make sure your non-swinging leg is slightly bent – this will help maintain balance.

Swing your leg for a minute or two and notice how the feeling in one leg is very different from that in the other.

Reverse swinging legs and repeat the practice.

Resume the grounded position.

Powerful Breathing

The leader says:

Standing in the grounded position, focus your attention on your breathing. Breathe in through your nose and out through your mouth.

With your arms loose by your sides, slowly raise your hands upward to a point at your lower ribs, middle fingers touching at their tips, palms facing up and horizontal to the floor. As you bend your arms, inhale through the nose. Breathe in at the same time as raising your arms – one action (raising your arms) will support the other (your in-breath). You may notice that as you inhale in this manner your abdomen fills with air. This is correct. Repeat this form of breathing several times.

Relax, letting your arms loosen. Resume the grounded position.

The leader says:

Slowly push downwards with your hands, middle fingers touching at their tips, palms facing down and horizontal to the floor. As you exert more pressure down your arms into your hands exhale through your mouth. Use the downward force with your arms to push air from your lungs out your mouth – one action (lowering your arms) will support the other (your out-breath). You might release a puffing or hissing sound with this movement. This is fine. Again, exhaling like this contracts your abdomen. Repeat this form of breathing several times.

Relax, letting your arms loosen. Resume the grounded position.

The leader says:

Now we put these two practices together. So...breathe in through your nose, raising your hands to your lower ribs [the leader demonstrates], *turn your palms over so that they are facing down, and breathe out through your mouth, pushing downwards until your arms are fully outstretched* [the leader demonstrates]. *This is powerful breathing.*

Practise powerful breathing until the group feels comfortable and confident with it.

Strolling Powerfully

The group strolls freely around the room until the leader calls out '*stop*', then '*take your grounded position*', at which point members anchor their feet to the surface. Then the leader calls '*powerful breathing*', at which point the members breathe in and out a few times using the above method.

This is practised until the group feels comfortable and confident.

Chinese Boxing

In a grounded position, partners face each other at about a metre's distance. They outstretch both arms halfway, meeting their partner's palms. Hold this position.

The aim of this game is to off-balance your opponent by pushing against their palms. As soon as your opponent moves one foot, the other wins. Pulling away your own hands, so that your opponent hits air and probably loses his balance, is encouraged.

By sifting winners and losers every couple of minutes it is possible to have a whole-group competition. Less successful members can model themselves on others' successes.

Session 12

MINDFUL BREATHING MEDITATION

Practise Mindful Breathing Meditation for 10 to 15 minutes.

While meditating the group leader can read the following. It is an extract from *The Buddha's Ancient Path* (Piyadassi 1964), a book that describes the fundamentals of Buddhism, including Buddhist psychology. When the meditation is concluded the group might like to discuss the extract.

The leader reads:

When you practise concentration on in- and out-breathing, you should fix your attention at the point where the moving air strokes the nostrils and note how breath goes in and out, but do not follow it. There should not be any holding or stopping of your breath. It should be quite natural without any effort or force on your part. At times it may become so fine that you may no longer notice it. When you go on developing this mindfulness by degrees, and when your mind is fully concentrated on the breath, you will notice that there is only a breath and nothing behind the scenes – no Self, Soul, ego or anything of that nature – that is, the breath and you are not two things, there is only a process. If you can come to that level, your concentration is very high, and with this comes rapturous joy, calm and peace of mind, but this may be only for a short moment, and your mind may again become discursive, your thoughts may wander and you may find it difficult to concentrate. It does not matter, you should 'onwards ever bravely press …[7] (Piyadassi 1964, p.215)

MOVEMENT: UPPER BODY – STRIKING

Arm and Heel-Lifting Breathing

The group stands either in a spacious circle, or as individuals scattered in a room, facing the same direction.

The leader says:

Stand in the grounded position and focus your attention on your breathing with your mouth slightly open.

Raise your arms from by your sides to about shoulder height and, while raising them up, lift your heels from the ground, straightening your knees, so that you are standing on your toes. When I say 'drop', relax your arms (letting them fall back by your sides) and your heels (so that you are again standing flat on the ground).

This is practised a few times. The group will notice that when the arms and heels are raised the breath draws in and the abdomen expands (inhalation), and when the arms and heels are lowered the breath is exhaled and the abdomen contracts.

Now this time when you raise your arms and heels keep them up for a moment or two, and when you relax them push air from your lungs out your mouth. You might release a puffing or hissing sound with this movement. This is fine. Repeat this several times.

Relax, letting your arms loosen. Resume the grounded position.

Powerful Breathing Voice

Group members lie on their bellies and prepare to do arm push-ups. This means that they can push from their bended knees if they find full push-ups difficult. As they push away from the ground the leader points out that there is an involuntary exhalation of air from their mouths. The group can exaggerate this sound (puffing, hissing, etc.). It is important that they develop their own powerful breathing voice.

Small groups of three are formed. Two group members place their hands on the shoulders of the third member who is in the middle. They keep their hands there as this person squats, slowly bending his knees with a straight back. Then he pushes up quickly (explosively) with his legs, exhaling air from his mouth with a cry. This cry gives him added strength. It is his powerful breathing voice.

Striking Position

The leader says:

Go to your grounded position but move your legs wider apart by taking a small step sideways with one foot. If you are right-handed move your left foot; if you are left-handed move your right foot.

As your body-weight follows this sideways movement turn your body slightly and face that direction making your hands into fists. If you are right-handed your left fist will be up and forward, ready to protect your face and your right fist will be held back and slightly lower, in front of your chest, ready to strike from this position. If you are left-handed your right fist will be forward, ready to protect your face and your left fist will be held back.

This is your striking position, and one you will return to in mock combat. Become comfortable with it.

The group repeats the change from grounded position to striking position until they feel comfortable with this new position.

Jabbing

The group moves into a spacious circle facing inwards. They take their striking position.

The leader says:

You are now going to jab with your forward fist, and as you do so step onto your forward leg so that your body-weight is transferred in the same direction as your forward-jabbing fist. Notice that you will exhale air from your mouth as you jab forward. This is fine.

Ensure that when making a fist, the fingers are bent to the maximum and that the thumb is bent over them. Keep the wrist straight. When the arm is extended the first two knuckles strike the target – this won't damage the weaker third and fourth knuckles. Each outgoing movement is supported with an exhalation. The pelvis always moves smoothly. Keep the back foot solidly but flexibly grounded.

When you have extended your jab return your arm and fist to your striking position. This return movement is called 'recovery'.

Now the group practises 'jabbing–recovering', the leader demonstrating: *'jab–recover; jab–recover; jab–recover'.*

Then each group member does a single 'jab–recover' around the circle, like a Mexican wave. Remember that with each jab there should be a powerful exhalation.

Finally, under the leader's direction, the group moves back to their striking position, then their grounded position, then they relax.

Striking

The leader says:

Jab and recover with your forward arm and fist then do the same with your attacking arm and fist so that the blow with the leading fist is short and supported by the pelvis and that the blow with the attacking fist, which travels a longer distance, is powerful and well directed. Practise this thoroughly, slowly at first then increasing in speed.

The group might discuss the differences they feel in delivering these strikes – their speed and force. Also, how does the exhalation of breath affect the strength of each blow?

Now practise this combination of leading and attacking strikes in the following drills:

- 2 times leading fist, 1 time attacking fist
- 2 times leading fist, 2 times attacking fist
- 3 times leading fist, 1 time attacking fist
- 4 times leading fist, 1 time attacking fist.

Combinations such as these, as determined by the group leader, are practised thoroughly.

Reverse-Fist Striking

The leader says:

This time we are going through the striking practice again but now we are reversing our normal handedness. So if you are right-handed you will now punch as if you are left-handed, and if you are left-handed you will now punch as if you are right-handed.

So...go to your grounded position but move your legs wider apart by taking a small step sideways with one foot. If you are right-handed move your right foot; if you are left-handed move your left foot. As your body-weight follows this sideways step turn your body, facing that direction and making your hands into fists. If you are right-handed your right fist will be leading, ready to protect your face, and your left fist will be held slightly lower, in front of your chest, ready to strike from this position. If you are left-handed your left fist will be leading, ready to protect your face, and your right fist will be held slightly lower, in front of your chest, ready to attack.

This is your reverse-fist striking position.

The group repeats the change from grounded position to reverse-fist striking position.

They then repeat the drills outlined above.

Session 13

MINDFUL BREATHING MEDITATION

Practise Mindful Breathing Meditation for 10 to 15 minutes.

When you have finished the leader says:

In this part of the session you will learn how to end your meditation successfully.

But before you do this you must decide how long you want each meditation to last. Somewhere around 15 to 20 minutes is suggested. It is up to you as a group member – depending on your personal, and the group's, circumstances.

This needs to be discussed by the group. Individuals meditating outside the group can regulate their own schedules.

To end your meditation, try to return to your usual wakeful consciousness slowly. Give yourself time to readjust to wakeful life. Try not to hurry. Open your eyes after you are fully conscious.

You might want to conclude with one or two stretches.

Finally, it's a good idea not to start talking immediately. Be reflective for a minute or two and respectful of others' readjustments.

In his handbook *Meditation: The Buddhist Way of Tranquility and Insight* (1992) Kamalashila puts it this way:

> *When you are ready, gently bring the practice to an end. Bring it to an end gradually: slowly open your eyes, and sit quietly for a while before getting up. Don't get up too abruptly, even if you feel like doing something energetic straight away, because that could easily jar your mood – it may perhaps make you over-sensitive later on in the day.*
>
> *It is important to make a smooth transition from a session of meditation to the rest of the day – don't immediately get involved with the hustle and bustle but do something quietly, just for a few minutes. Gaze out of the window, take a short stroll, make a hot drink – do something reflective that will help you to assimilate the experience, even if nothing special seems to have happened in the meditation.*
>
> *Remember that the way a session of meditation has affected you may not be obvious all at once...* (Kamalashila 1992, p.19)

MOVEMENT: UPPER BODY – BLOCKING

The following instructions are for both left and right-handed people. They can be practised with a partner once you've mastered them by yourself.

Simple High Block ('Wiping')

This is used to protect yourself from blows to the face.

The leader says:

Bend your right arm and hold up your fist up high, in front of the right side of your face. Bring your left fist across your chest.

Now swing your left arm outwards and upwards in an arc, stopping your fist in front of the left side of your face, and as you do so, bring your right fist down across your chest. This is rather like windscreen wipers.

This parrying, deflective movement is repeated with both arms. Practise slowly at first then more powerfully until the arms are working fluently together.

Simple Middle Block ('Chopping')

This is to protect from chest and stomach blows. It uses a chopping motion.

The leader says:

Bend your right arm (palms inwards, wrist straight, fist clenched) and hold it level with the side of your body and bring your left fist across your chest.

Swing your left fist outward and downward in an arc, across the front of your body, stopping when it is level with the left side of your body, and as you do so, bring your right fist up across your chest. This is a chopping movement.

Repeat this until the arms can swing powerfully together.

Simple Low Block ('Sweeping')

This block is used to deflect a kick or punch away from the lower part of your body. It is a sweeping motion.

The leader says:

Begin with the same position as Simple Middle Block – with your right arm bent at the side of your body and your left arm across your chest.

Now move your right fist up a little then downwards in a circular motion across your body, striking with the outside edge of your arm. Complete the sweep over your right knee.

Then, swing your left fist down across your body to your left knee, and as you do so, bring your right fist back across your body to your chest. This is a sweeping motion.

Practise this until both arms are working together, sweeping alternately across the body.

Practising Together

Practise these moves carefully with a partner, standing apart, a few centimetres further than your outstretched striking range.

At first practise them in slow-motion, ensuring that every part of the move is correct and secure.

For the Simple High Block the partner strikes from overhead; the Simple Middle Block the partner strikes chest and body; for Simple Low Block the partner strikes below the waist with strikes or kicks.

Practising this will necessitate both partners revisiting the Striking exercises learned in the last session.

Session 14

MINDFUL BREATHING MEDITATION

Meditation takes many different forms: reciting a mantra, focusing visually on an object (such as a candle), walking (as in 'walking meditation'), pondering riddle-evoking questions, meditating with different breathing practices, and so on. But generally speaking meditation cultivates either serenity (*samatha*) (sometimes called 'calmness') or insight (*vipassana*) (sometimes called 'mindfulness'). Those forms of meditation that develop serenity emphasize the 'slowing down' and restorative effects of meditation. In order to experience this the meditator focuses his or her mind upon an object or practice, allowing the mind to become 'absorbed' into it. Often awareness is set aside. Relaxation exercises and visualizations are examples of serenity-evoking practices.

Insight meditation is more concerned with what is brought to the consciousness of the mind – what it 'sees'. Here the mind's content and processes are explored, including its limitless capacity for distraction. The meditator brings into his or her mind an enquiring awareness, accompanied by an acute alertness to what is here and now before the mind. Examples of insight meditation are Vipassana Meditation, recently introduced into the West by S.N. Goenka (see Hart 1987) and the Mahasi method, originally taught by Mahasi Sayadaw in Burma during the second part of the twentieth century (see Kearney 2001).

The form of meditation we have learned is 'Anapana' (*anapana sati*), meaning 'mindfulness of breathing'. According to Buddhist teaching, this was the first topic on meditation expounded by the Buddha in his *Great Discourse on the Foundations of Mindfulness* (see Ariyadhamma 1988). Mindful Breathing Meditation blends serenity and insight – the calming qualities of in and out-breathing provides deep rest; our alertness to the breath's contact with the nostrils brings consciousness to our thoughts and emotions as they arise 'here' and 'now'. Goenka recommends Mindful Breathing Meditation as preparatory to practising Vipassana Meditation.

A slight variation of this form of meditation is described in the following extract from *Yoga, Tantra and Meditation* (1976) by Swami Janakananda Saraswati. In this book it is called Little Deep Relaxation. The group might like to experience this meditation, comparing it with what we have learned. The text is to be read as a verbal instruction.

The leader reads:

...Notice air passing through your nose. Notice air passing in and out of the nostrils.

Try not to influence your breathing at all but observe this natural breathing process. Natural breathing in and out of the nose. Concentrate on this a while. Absolute natural breathing. Don't change it. Try not to give it any kind of tempo. It looks after itself and you observe it.

Imagine that the air goes in through one nostril and out the other, in the other and out the first; alternate breathing in one nostril and out the other, in the other and out the first. Always inhale through the nostril through which you have just exhaled. Go on with this.

In one nostril, out the other, in the other, out the first. Don't use your finger, imagine it all.

And then start counting. When you inhale through one nostril, say ***one*** *(silently to yourself), out through the other;* ***one****; in through the other;* ***two****, out through the first;* ***two****, inhale through the first;* ***three****, out through the other;* ***three****, in through the other;* ***four****, out through the first;* ***four****.*

When you come to the fifth, inhale through both nostrils and exhale again through both.

Six*, in through the first again;* ***six****, out through the other;* ***seven****, in through the other,* ***seven****, out through the first;* ***eight****, in through the first;* ***eight****, out through the other;* ***nine****, in through the other;* ***nine****, out through the first;* ***ten****, in through both nostrils;* ***ten****, out through both nostrils;* ***eleven****, in through one;* ***eleven****, out through the other. Keep this up.*

Go on counting...and at 5, 10, 15, 20, 25, 30, etc.: in through both nostrils, out through both. Otherwise alternate, in through one, out through the other, in through the other, out through the first.

Go on counting and try to get as far as possible without making a mistake. If you forget to use both nostrils every fifth time, if you fall asleep or count incorrectly, start over. Begin again with ***one****, as soon as you discover that you have made a mistake. Try not to make a mistake, try to count as high as you can. Do this a good long time. Careful counting. Conscious counting and conscious breathing...* (Saraswati 1976, p.89)

The leader says:

We will conclude this part of the session with some Mindful Breathing Meditation of our own. Remember what we learned in our last session about how to end our meditation successfully.

MOVEMENT: LOWER BODY – KICKING

Simple Front Kick

This kick follows the natural walking movement of the body. When executing it with bare feet, ensure that you use the ball of your foot or your heel (for low targets), with the toes curled back – so that they do not get damaged in contact.

The leader says:

Stand in your grounded position. Lift your right knee straight up, and as it reaches its highest point snap your foot forward. Keep your fists in front of you to guard your body, letting them fall to your sides after striking. When you've made contact do not let your foot drop to the floor, but bring it back to its knee-up position. Then place your foot on the floor.

Repeat this with the left knee and foot.

Practise alternate right and left front kicking, slowly at first then more powerfully.

Simple Side Kick

The leader says:

As with the Simple Front Kick, stand in your grounded position and lift your right knee straight up. But now rotate your body to your left, shifting your weight to your standing leg. (Ensure that it is bent sufficiently to maintain your balance.)

Then, from this position, thrust your leg out to the side, kicking to the height of your ribs. Make contact with your heel or outer edge of the foot. The strength of this kick comes from the power of your weight as you rotate your body and drive your foot outwards.

After completing the kick, face frontward and return the right foot to its knee-up position. Then place the foot on the floor.

Throughout this move keep your fists in front of you to guard your body, letting them fall to your sides after striking.

Repeat this with your left leg and foot.

Practise alternate right and left side kicking, slowly at first then more powerfully.

MOVEMENT: LOWER BODY – BLOCKING

Simple Knee Block

The leader says:

You may use your legs to block a fist or kicking attack.

In the event of an oncoming attack, raise your knee (right or left) parallel to the floor and allow your upper leg muscles to absorb the strike or kick. This defensive position can quickly be turned into an attacking one by either executing a simple front kick or (when your opponent is at close range) raising your knee higher to a knee kick.

Simple Foot Block

The leader says:

You may use your feet to block or deflect kicks.

In the event of an oncoming low kick, snap your foot (left or right) upward and inward from the floor. This will strike at your attacker's leg, deflecting the kick.

Alternatively, before the kick begins, thrust the side edge of your foot (left or right) against your opponent's ankle. This will unbalance your opponent, giving you the advantage.

Practising Together

Practise in pairs all of the above moves – striking, kicking, parrying and blocking. Under the direction of the leader work on attack–defence drills, slowly at first (perhaps in slow-motion or half-speed) then, as confidence grows, increase in speed. Slow practice provides the chance to correct techniques. It also allows opportunities to use moves that you may not use in full speed encounters.

Always practise in light contact, as opposed to 'contact' or 'heavy-contact'. This means that while you may touch your opponent no injury will be caused.

Session 15: Review

MINDFUL BREATHING MEDITATION

The leader says:

This is our final session. It is a review in which we can revisit any of the Mindful Breathing Meditation practices we've experienced in other sessions.

The group can nominate a Meditation session they would like to repeat, or practise the form of Mindful Breathing Meditation we have learned.

MOVEMENT: UPPER BODY AND LOWER BODY

Review

The group can revisit any of the favoured Upper Body – Striking activities. These are:

- Arm and Heel-Lifting Breathing
- Powerful Breathing Voice
- Striking Position
- Jabbing
- Striking
- Reverse-Fist Striking.

Rooster Fighting

In this game strength, balance and control are all crucial.

In pairs, partners hold each other by the hand and then stand on one leg. The hands that hold can be locked in a monkey-grip, or similar. The other hand supports the free leg, holding onto the ankle.

By pulling, pushing and skipping on one leg, partners try to disturb each other's balance. Victory is signalled when the loser puts two feet on the ground.

After one or two games change legs.

As with Chinese Boxing, by sifting winners and losers every couple of minutes it is possible to have a whole-group competition. Less successful members can model themselves on others' successes.

Review

The group can revisit any of the favoured Upper Body – Blocking activities. These are:

- Simple High Block ('Wiping')
- Simple Middle Block ('Chopping')
- Simple Low Block ('Sweeping').

Bull Fighting

Partners face each other at about a metre's distance. The 'toreador' keeps his forearms (palms inwards, wrists straight, fists clenched) crossed vertically in front of him but away from his chest. The 'bull' has to push the toreador's arms against his chest.

To fend off the bull the toreador moves with the bull's pushes bending away with arm and footwork.

Ensure that the toreador keeps constant eye-contact with his opponent and maintains flexibility, self-control and balance.

It is possible to turn this game into a whole-group competition. As with Chinese Boxing and Rooster Fighting, sift winners and losers every couple of minutes.

Practise this until both arms are working together, sweeping alternatively across the body.

The group can revisit any of the favoured Lower Body – Kicking activities.

These are:

- Simple Front Kick
- Simple Side Kick.

Review

The group can revisit any of the favoured Lower Body – Blocking activities.

These are:

- Simple Knee Block
- Simple Foot Block.

Practising Together

Practise all the above moves carefully with a partner, standing apart, a few centimetres further than your outstretched striking range.

At first practise them in slow-motion, then in half-motion, ensuring that every part of the move is correct and secure.

Troubleshooting

MEDITATION

Despite its apparent straightforwardness most of us find meditation difficult to do, at least at first, and for some of us it isn't suitable, especially if we're feeling particularly anxious or depressed or generally not engaged with life. If we're feeling like this we'd probably be better off seeing a counsellor and coming back to meditation later. But for those of us trying to do some form of meditation and finding it difficult the following tips and advise might be useful.

Sitting Posture

A sitting posture that is good for meditation is sitting cross-legged on a cushion on the floor, relaxed and alert. The weight of you body should be balanced vertically over your buttocks with minimal muscular support. Arms and legs should be symmetrical. Hands can rest palm on top of palm, facing upwards.

A common fault in such sitting posture is over-arching or slumping in your back. Over-arching is when your spin arches inward too far – your upper pelvis is pushed forward while your tailbone and buttocks stick out. This puts a lot of strain on your lower back. To counter this lower your seat (cushion) and relax your lower back. Make sure that the height at which you are sitting feels right – your body should rest without strain and you should be self-supported. Slumping is the opposite – your upper pelvis is too far back and your tailbone is tucking under causing your lower back to collapse and your shoulders to slump. The remedy for this is to heighten your seat and straighten your back to its natural curve. Always treat your body with kindness and respect. Be firm with yourself but not punitive.

Tiredness

If we don't put enough energy into our meditation our mind feels dull and heavy and we may fall asleep. One way to combat this is to increase physical stimulation. This may mean opening our eyes when meditating, or turning on a light, opening a window and sitting in a draught, massaging our limbs, or pulling our earlobes – a traditional Zen method! Another strategy is to concentrate on our sitting posture, leaning slightly backwards so that our head can't bow forward and we won't have the opportunity to nod off to sleep.

What's important in this is to recognize our tiredness from the beginning. Once we've recognized it we can observe it, making it conscious, and therefore regaining control of our mindfulness.

Restlessness

Restlessness occurs when there is too much energy in our meditation. When this happens we become the victim of fidgeting or anxiety. There are two ways to counter this, the first more challenging than the second.

The first is popularly referred to as 'surfing the urge' and means that rather than ignoring or resisting feelings of worry and fear we go with them, riding their waves of agitation and stress. We try to concentrate on our thoughts and emotions as they arise in our mind, but rather than engaging in their content – letting them dominate our attention – we try to get outside of them (so to speak) and observe the process, watching them.

Less difficult than this, is resting our mind and diverting energy to our body. This is deliberately intended *not* to involve our thoughts and feelings but focus on our body's physical sensations and our reactions to them.

Distractions

The main hindrance to successful meditation is what's called 'distraction', which is when our mind wanders unnoticed from one sensory input (listening to a sound, feeling sensations on our skin, detecting tastes and smells, and so on) to another, from one thought to another, from one feeling to another, etc. What we mean to be attentive to – the here and now of our senses or mental activities – is lost to us. We become unobservant and unconscious and fail to *remind* ourselves that meditation is noticing processes, not becoming involved in content.

Once distractions are noticed, however, they cease to be distractions because we become aware of them in the present moment, and it is being conscious in the here and now that we are striving for.

Negativity

Sometimes in our meditation we can become preoccupied with negativity as certain thoughts and feelings upset us or won't go away. What seems to happen is that negative feelings from our everyday life – such as anger or blame or greed – arise in our meditation and we recall the pain of these experiences and become attached to them. Because our feelings are unresolved in our active life, when we meditate we can't seem to let them go. We are trapped in our resentments, and while this is going on it seems impossible to concentrate on anything else.

Practising loving kindness meditation is an ideal remedy to this. This is not only because the compassion of loving kindness counters negativity but because this meditation starts with us and our self-esteem. Once we can truly appreciate our own worth and uniqueness then we can radiate goodwill towards others.

Self-doubt

Our final hindrance to successful meditation is self-doubt. It arises as a crisis in confidence in what we are doing and why we are doing it – in this case meditating. Sometimes such doubt is entirely justified, such as when we are questioning the effectiveness of certain meditative practices or their theoretic basis or their relevance to our life. There is nothing wrong with these sincere doubts.

In other cases, however, we doubt things for the sake of doubting. During our meditation then we may become resistant and indecisive. We may hold back from committing to serious effort, or procrastinate. We may lose trust that we are making progress or benefiting from the practice.

Under some circumstances like these it might be best to cease meditating altogether and seek guidance from an experienced instructor. On the other hand we might want to simply relax and tune out (temporarily) from meditating. This may help reduce inner tension, restoring peacefulness and energy.

MOVEMENT

General Warm-Up Exercises

Before commencing any focused physical movement it is a good idea to warm up your muscles beforehand. Stressing tight muscles is the cause of most sports injuries.

Warm-ups are designed to increase your breathing and heart rates and raise the temperature of muscle tissue. A good indication of successful warming up is when you are slightly sweaty. Take about five to ten minutes for general warming up.

You might begin with a very light physical activity such as walking, jogging slowly on the spot or easy trampolining. Then, with your arms do some pumping and make large circular movements. Follow this with a brief lunge walk, keeping your chest up, looking straight ahead and co-ordinating your arms with your legs. This will loosen up your hips and strengthen your buttocks and hamstring muscles. Now alter your pose slightly by extending your body forwards and swinging your arms. Knee lifts (lifting each thigh to a position parallel to the ground) and calf-walks (extending your ankle in an exaggerated step) will improve hip and ankle flexibility and strengthen Achilles and calf tendons and muscles. Finally, do some sideways and backwards skipping and running. This too is good for lower limb agility.

Specific Warm-Up Exercises

Before commencing a specific exercise it is important to do warm-ups that are appropriate to that exercise and to do them immediately prior. In other words, don't warm up first in a generalized way, wait five or ten minutes or so, then do a specific exercise. Rather, prepare your body's particular neuromuscular patterning then move straight to the activity.

An excellent method for specific exercise preparation is to undertake the upcoming exercise at a slow pace or in slow motion. For example, in executing upper body exercises such as jabbing or striking it is advisable to practise these slowly at first, gradually increasing in speed and power. Always try to keep within the limits of your strength and responsiveness.

Stretches

Stretches are best performed after your body is warmed up. Perform light static stretching routines – in which you modestly stretch a muscle and hold it in its extended position for 10-30 seconds – within the limits of your comfort. Such stretches might include leaning and pushing against a wall, floor stretches and easy leg and arm bar twists.

More practised participants can carry out more exertive drill methods such as ballistic, dynamic or proprioceptive neuromuscular facilitation stretching. Routines for these include simulated movements, drives and severe stretches.

Cooling Down Exercises

Cooling down following exercise means gradually decreasing your level of activity. This allows your breathing and heart rates to return to normalcy and your body temperature to fall slowly. Take about five to ten minutes for overall cooling down. Effective cooling down will also help preventing delayed-onset muscle soreness.

Begin cooling down by slowing the pace and exertion of your last activity. That is, gradually decrease the strenuousness of your final exercise until you can comfortably perform it in slow motion. When you've achieved this perform in reverse the routines practised for warming up, ending with a slow jog or brisk walk. Try to ensure that every activity in cooling down is lower in intensity than the previous.

Conclusion

This program introduces students to meditation, therapeutic games and writing and talking, and to some basic skills in the martial arts. Through this it strengthens students' self-control, resilience and respect.

To maximize benefit, however, the skills learned in this program must be practised routinely. The program is a starting point in exploring meditation and disciplined movement. It is preliminary to more sophisticated forms of meditation (such as Vipassana as understood by S.N. Goenka) and codified martial arts.

Though perhaps not truly a 'therapy', the effects of Mindful Breathing Meditation can be therapeutic. Following Buddhism's Eightfold Path to Awakening, effective meditation is considered to have three main aspects:

1. 'right effort' (*samma vayama*), which is the **energy** demanded by a task; how we intend to engage in it; our distinction between what we believe is helpful and unhelpful
2. 'right mindfulness' (*samma sati*), which is the **awareness** we bring to an object and the precision we give to the *here* and *now*
3. 'right concentration' (*samma samadhi*), which is our **focus** upon an object; our 'absorption', as it were, into it.

These attributes come together uniquely in Mindful Breathing Meditation to offer the practitioner:

- an effective **diversion** from anxiety or other mental ailments. While focusing on the flow of air at the nostrils the meditator can be drawn away from disturbances and internal stressors
- a tool for the meditator to **surf the urge** for resuming unwanted behaviours. Mindful Breathing enables the participant to experience (even confront) undesired thoughts, feelings and urges while remaining occupied, distanced and in some manner detached from them
- a technique for **de-identifying** with our subjectivity. When we sense closely our in and out breath at the nostrils we identify this point as both 'I' and 'not I' since we are both at the breath and its observer. Experientially, this creates a space between us and our responses. This enables de-identification with inner stresses.

This characterization of Mindful Breathing Meditation can be contrasted with relaxation exercises and visualizations. In relaxation exercises energy is dispersed throughout the body, and it is the body that the mind strongly focuses upon. Emphasis is given to calmness, restoration and rejuvenation. In visualizations focus is again important but now the mind is alerted to inner fantasies and narratives. The resultant calmness depends on the strength of the meditator's imagination. Both relaxation and visualizations tend to set aside consciousness to thoughts and emotions. Mindful Breathing Meditation, on the other hand, requires a subtle balancing of effort, awareness and focus.

Effective meditation of all forms is enhanced by a vigorous and healthy body, and for beginners, practising some basic martial arts techniques is about developing physical strength, flexibility, stamina and balance. From this an aesthetic appreciation often develops – the martial arts can be as graceful as they are skilled and as deft and fluid as they are energetic and powerful.

But we can also learn from the martial arts – especially from those known as the 'soft' or 'internal' Martial Arts[8] – about how to live in the world. We learn about:

- **grounding** – feeling 'grounded' is standing firm yet relaxed
- **powerful breathing** – which is energizing the body through abdominal breathing
- **walking powerfully** – centring our body awareness and sharpening our reactions to external commands
- **powerful voice** – which transmits mental activity to physical power

- **body equilibrium** – the balancing of the immovable rock attitude and the communicative water attitude.

This last concept (developed by Ykema 2000) can be applied at various levels. In terms of **combat** it means that an attack may be blocked or parried by firmly strained muscles (rock) or by moving with the attacker's force and turning it against them (water). (We practised this in the Bull Fighting exercise, for example.) At a **communication** level it can be seen in our attitude to social interaction, when we can be assertive (rock) or compliant (water) – with an inevitably different outcome. (We saw this in the Chinese Boxing exercise, for example.) And in terms of overall **consciousness**, the diligent participant finally gains the perspective that *both* rock and water are needed in different ways to reach self-fulfilment. This understanding is an ultimate goal of the program.

Movement and meditation are taught separately in these sessions but eventually they must be brought together. Movement brings meditation into our everyday lives, linking the physical with the mental, skills learned from one practice transferring to and enhancing the other.

Meditation and movement exercises are not seen as unconnected (perhaps esoterically) from the world but integrated into our experience of it. They nourish our wellbeing so that so that our living is empowered and enriched.

Endnotes

1 I've chosen this title as a tribute to a wonderful essay on meditation in Paul R. Fleischman's *Karma and Chaos: New and Collected Essays on Vipassana Meditation* (1999). The essay is 'Why I Sit' (1982).

2 The Mindful Breathing sections in the early sessions of this book owe considerably to a number of sources, – fore-mostly the Classic Buddhist text *Satipatthana Sutta* (*The Great Discourse on the Foundations of Mindfulness*), which is an account of the Buddha's exposition of the virtues of in-and-out breathing. I also owe to M.N. Ariyadhamma, *Anapana Sati: Meditation on Breathing* (1988), Kamalashila, *Meditation: The Buddhist Way of Tranquility and Insight* (1992), Ven. Analayo, *Satipatthana: The Direct Path to Realization* (2003) and many other sources.

3 This is one of many psychodramatic and therapeutic play activities for children and adolescents described in K.N. Dwivedi's (ed.) *Group Work with Children and Adolescents: A Handbook* (1993) and elsewhere.

4 Theatre sports is a great source of therapeutic activities and games. A list of theatre sports is available on the web at: www.whitman.edu/theatre_sports/index.html

5 Well known examples of Relaxation, Visualization and other forms of 'stress management' and 're-focusing' music and recordings of natural sounds are Susan Kramer, *Meditation for all Kids* (2000) (some texts by Susan Kramer are available at: Guided Meditation for Children: www.susankramer.com/ChildMeditation.html); F. Adrigan, P. Conlon and M. Willis, *Keeping Cool, Keeping Calm: Ways to Relax and Manage Stress for 6–12-year-olds*; and Debbie Goodall, *Mystical Moments*, which comprises a single music/sounds track without voice-over.

6 In the following Movement sections I have borrowed practices and suggestions from many martial arts sources. I am also indebted to Freerk Ykema's *Rock and Water: Working with Boys, Building Fine Men: An Educational Programme Centred Around Safety and Integrity*

(2000). A DVD is also available: *Rock and Water: Basic Exercises Skills for Physical–Social Teaching for Boys.*

7 The Buddha's Eightfold Path to Awakening outlines the way Buddhist enlightenment may be attained. It is preserved in the *Dhammacakkappavattana Sutta* and contains the mental disciplines 'right effort', 'right mindfulness' and 'right concentration'. An excellent discussion of the Eightfold Path to Awakening is Bhikkhu Bodhi's *The Noble Eightfold Path: The Way to the End of Suffering* at: www.accesstoinsight.org/lib/authors/bodhi/waytoend.html

8 For a clear, sensitive and informative discussion of practices and philosophies of the main 'soft style' or 'internal' Martial Arts see Paul Brecher, *The Way of the Spiritual Warrior* (1998).

References

Adrigan, F., Conlon, P. and Willis, M. *Keeping Cool, Keeping Calm: Ways to Relax and Manage Stress for 6–12-Year-Olds* (CD-Rom), produced by Greg Tuchin. Sydney: Sydney South West Area Health Service: NSW Health.

Analayo, Venerable (2003) *Satipatthana: The Direct Path to Realization.* Birmingham: Windhorse Publications.

Ariyadhamma, M.N. (1988) 'Anapana Sati: Meditation on Breathing'. *Bodhi Leaves 115.* Kandy: Buddhist Publication Society. Available at: www.accesstoinsight.org/lib/authors/ariyadhamma/bl115.html, accessed 27 November 2008.

Bodhi, B. (1984) 'The Noble Eightfold Path'. *The Wheel 308/311.* Kandy: Buddhist Publication Society. Available at: www.accesstoinsight.org/lib/authors/bodhi/waytoend.html, accessed 27 November 2008.

Brecher, P. (1998) *The Way of the Spiritual Warrior.* New York: Godsfield Press.

Dwivedi, K.N. (ed.) (1993) *Group Work with Children and Adolescents: A Handbook.* London: Jessica Kingsley Publishers.

Fleischman, P.R. (1999) *Karma and Chaos: New and Collected Essays on Vipassana Meditation.* Seattle, WA: Vipassana Research Publications.

Goodall, D. (2007) *Mystical Moments* (CD Rom). Available at www.relaxnpeace.com/index.html, accessed 27 November 2008.

Hart, W. (1987) *The Art of Living: Vipassana Meditation: As Taught by S.N. Goenka.* San Francisco, CA: Harper & Row.

Kamalashila (1992) *Meditation: The Buddhist Way of Tranquility and Insight.* Birmingham: Windhorse Publications.

Kearney, P. (2001) 'Serene and clear: An introduction to Buddhist meditation: Week six: The Mahasi Method.' Available at: www.meditation.asn.au/Documents/Serene2001/06%20The%20Mahasi%20method, accessed 27 November 2008.

Piyadassi, T. (1964) *The Buddha's Ancient Path.* Taipei: ROC.

Saraswati, S.J. (1976). *Yoga, Tantra and Meditation.* New York: Ballantine Books. Strength and Difficulties Questionnaire available at www.sdqinfo.com, accessed 27 November 2008. Theatre Sports available at www.whitman.edu/theatre_sports/index.html, accessed 27 November 2008.

Ykema, F. (c. 2000) *Rock and Water: Working with Boys, Building Fine Men: An Educational Programme Centred around Safety and Integrity.* University of Newcastle, Callaghan, NSW, Australia; The Family Action Centre. A DVD is also available: *Rock and Water: Basic Exercises Skills for Phsyical–Social Teaching for Boys.* Amsterdam: GADAKU Institute Netherlands BOOZ – Audiovisuele Produktie, available in Australia from The Family Action Centre, University of Newcastle, Callaghan, NSW.

Further Reading

This book draws material from a number of sources. Following the Theravadic tradition of Buddhism it adopts a practical, experiential approach to meditation that is based directly on the teachings of the Buddha. Some of these teachings have recently been gathered by John Holder into a single volume that is easily accessible to students (*Early Buddhist Discourses,* 2006, Indianapolis, IN: Hackett Publishing Co., Inc.). Among the teachings here are the Buddha's 'Great Discourse on the Foundations of Mindfulness' and his key discourses on religious attitudes and philosophic positions. The complete account of the Buddha's teachings is in the *Sutta Pitaka* (Discourse Basket) of the Pali Canon, which is a multi-volume collection of sermons and instructions of the Buddha and his disciples.

General works on the Buddha and Buddhism abound. Two in particular are recommended here, Kamalashila's *Meditation: The Buddhist Way of Tranquility and Insight* (1992, Birmingham: Windhorse Publications), a down-to-earth but academic text that covers Buddhist meditative practices and theory, and Paul Fleischman's *Karma and Chaos: New and Collected Essays on Vipassana Meditation* (1999, Seattle, WA: Vipassana Research Publications), a much more personalized account of meditating. Beyond this, the inquiring reader will find a wealth of information and insight in books such as Richard Gombrich's *Theravada Buddhism* (1988, London: Routledge and Kegan Paul), Peter Harvey's *An Introduction to Buddhism* (1990, Cambridge: Cambridge University Press), I.B. Horner's *The Early Buddhist Theory of Man Perfected* (1936, London: Williams and Norgate) and works by David Kalupahana, Sangharakshita, Thera Piyadassi or Thich Nhat Hanh.

Useful Buddhist organizations and websites too are plentiful. A directory of different organizations in Australasia, the UK and the USA (by regions rather than nation) is available on the internet via 'The Buddhist Directory' (in your search engine), while some of the best known websites are: www.buddhanet.net, an information network advertising a variety of meditation techniques, teachings and events information, as well as a world directory, www.dharmanet.org, which has information on Buddhist organizations from different traditions, and www.ciolek.com/WWWVL-Buddhism.html, which is a virtual library providing listings of information facilities in Buddhism and Buddhist studies.

Another source this book draws on is related to the martial arts, particularly those known as the 'soft' or 'internal' style. This stresses consciousness of internal energy and control rather than external combat. Paul Brecher's *The Way of the Spiritual Warrior* (1998, New York: Godsfield Press) or Zhongwen Fu's *Mastering Yang Style Taijiquan* (2006, Berkeley, CA: Blue Snake Books) are recommended as introductions to this field, both works being clear, instructive and comprehensive. Tai Chi classics that might also be consulted are Barbara Davis' *The Taijiquan Classics: An Annotated Translation* (2004, Berkeley, CA: North Atlantic Press) and Wile Doug's *Tai Chi Touchstones: Yang Family Secret Transmissions* (1983, New York: Sweet Ch'i Press) and *Lost T'ai-chi Classics from the Late Ch'ing Dynasty* (1996, Albany, NY: Suny Press). While there are numerous contacts available through the internet, joining a local gym or academy or martial arts class is probably the most expedient way to gain experience and confidence in this form of movement. National martial arts directories (for Australasia, the UK and the USA) are available on the web.

The book also draws material on movement from another source, that of therapeutic games and play activities often connected with psychodrama or theatre sports. Kedar Dwivedi's *Group Work with Children and Adolescents: A Handbook* (1993, London: Jessica Kingsley Publishers) is an excellent resource in this regard, providing history, theory, analysis and practices for those interested in how young people interact. It also pulls together different therapeutic approaches in this field, such as those of J.L. Moreno (*Psychodrama*, 1948, New York: Beacon House), Eric Berne (*Games People Play*, 1964, Harmondsworth: Penguin), Carl Rogers (*Encounter Groups*, 1973, London: Pelican-Penguin) and F.S. Perls (*Gestalt Therapy Integrated*, 1974, New York: Vintage Books), all of whom offer models and strategies in dealing with conflict, establishing empathy, learning to trust, being assertive, showing positive regard, and so on. To this list of texts must be added Freerk Ykema's Rock and Water program (2000, *Rock and Water: working with boys, building fine men: an educational program centred around Safety and Integrity*, Callaghan, NSW: Australia: University of Newcastle), which articulates the notion and practice of emotive and physical equilibrium.

Worksheets

WORKSHEET 1: SELF-ASSESSMENT QUIZ

Think about how you generally see yourself and what personal qualities you think you have.

Rate yourself against the following statements (0 = not at all; 2–3 = sometimes; 5 = all the time).

Generally speaking, I am honest.

0 1 2 3 4 5

Mostly, I am co-operative.

0 1 2 3 4 5

I am usually reliable.

0 1 2 3 4 5

I think I am popular.

0 1 2 3 4 5

I am friendly in most circumstances.

0 1 2 3 4 5

On the whole, I think I am kind.

0 1 2 3 4 5

I believe I am adventurous.

0 1 2 3 4 5

I usually feel I am confident.

0 1 2 3 4 5

WORKSHEET 2: MY FEELINGS, WHEN…

Think about how you have felt at certain times and in certain situations. Complete each of the following as best you can.

I feel *happy* when
*
*
*

I feel *sad* when
*
*
*

I feel *angry* when
*
*
*

I feel *calm* when
*
*
*

I feel *guilty* when
*
*
*

I feel *ashamed* when
*
*
*

I feel *pleased* when
*
*
*

WORKSHEET 3: MOOD QUIZ

Think about how you have felt over the past week or so.

Rate yourself against the following statements (0 = not at all; 5 = quite often; 10 = all the time).

Mostly, I have been happy.

0 1 2 3 4 5 6 7 8 9 10

I have been worried quite a lot.

0 1 2 3 4 5 6 7 8 9 10

I have felt bad-tempered.

0 1 2 3 4 5 6 7 8 9 10

I have felt liked by others.

0 1 2 3 4 5 6 7 8 9 10

I have felt different from others.

0 1 2 3 4 5 6 7 8 9 10

I have been sad or depressed.

0 1 2 3 4 5 6 7 8 9 10

I have been frightened.

0 1 2 3 4 5 6 7 8 9 10

I have generally felt positive.

0 1 2 3 4 5 6 7 8 9 10

WORKSHEET 4A: MOOD QUIZ VOCABULARY

(Juniors)

Think about how you are feeling now.

Listed below are some words that might describe your state of mind. Tick any that you feel apply to you.

- ☐ **sad**
- ☐ **tearful**
- ☐ **shocked**
- ☐ **hurt**
- ☐ **angry**
- ☐ **confused**
- ☐ **frightened**
- ☐ **stressed**
- ☐ **afraid**
- ☐ **relieved**
- ☐ **happy**
- ☐ **free**
- ☐ **shy**
- ☐ **ashamed**
- ☐ **guilty**
- ☐ **disappointed**
- ☐ **lazy**
- ☐ **annoyed**
- ☐ **moody**
- ☐ **calm**

WORKSHEET 4B: MOOD QUIZ VOCABULARY

(Seniors)

Think about how you are feeling now.

Listed below are some words that might describe your state of mind. Tick any that you feel apply to you.

- ☐ **sad**
- ☐ **tearful**
- ☐ **shocked**
- ☐ **hurt**
- ☐ **bitter**
- ☐ **angry**
- ☐ **outraged**
- ☐ **uncertain**
- ☐ **frightened**
- ☐ **anxious**
- ☐ **fearful**
- ☐ **confused**
- ☐ **perplexed**
- ☐ **chaotic**
- ☐ **relieved**
- ☐ **ashamed**
- ☐ **annoyed**
- ☐ **guilty**
- ☐ **disappointed**
- ☐ **moody**
- ☐ **apathetic**
- ☐ **lazy**
- ☐ **powerless**
- ☐ **redundant**
- ☐ **resilient**
- ☐ **inspired**
- ☐ **happy**
- ☐ **free**
- ☐ **argumentative**
- ☐ **calm**
- ☐ **carefree**
- ☐ **shy**
- ☐ **irresponsible**
- ☐ **excited**

WORKSHEET 5: FRIENDSHIP QUIZ

Think about how you behave as a friend and what skills you have in building and keeping friendships.

Rate yourself against the following statements (0 = not at all; 2–3 = sometimes; 5 = all the time).

I usually listen properly to my friends.

0 1 2 3 4 5

I try to respect their attitudes, beliefs and feelings.

0 1 2 3 4 5

I am mostly honest with them about my own views and feelings.

0 1 2 3 4 5

I can often motivate my friends to do their best.

0 1 2 3 4 5

I can support them when they feel sad or depressed.

0 1 2 3 4 5

I respect that my friends are different to me in some ways.

0 1 2 3 4 5

I can mostly cope with them having other friends.

0 1 2 3 4 5

I can cope with them being on their own sometimes.

0 1 2 3 4 5

WORKSHEET 6: MAKING A SOCIOGRAM

Make a sociogram, mapping your friendship circle(s).

The key feature of a sociogram is that it shows how individuals are connected.

Here are two models. The first is a diagram of circles (you and your friends – write names inside the circles) connected with lines.

The second represents a group of five students: one person prefers to be friendly with two others, but not friendly with the other two.

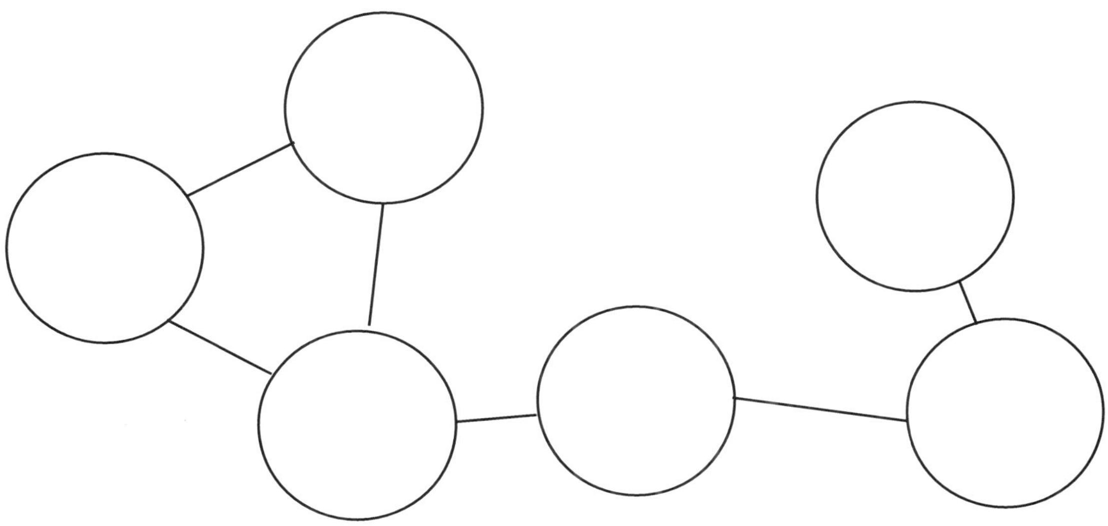

Preferred friendship: —————— Not preferred friendship: ---------

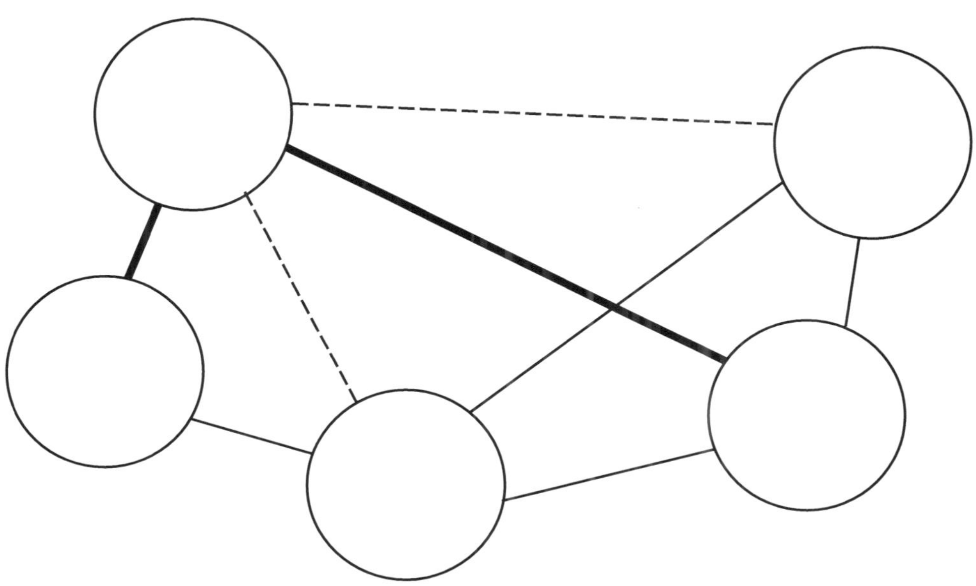

WORKSHEET 7: AFFIRMATIONS (1)

We are all good at something. Think about some of the things you are good at and jot them down in the balloons below.

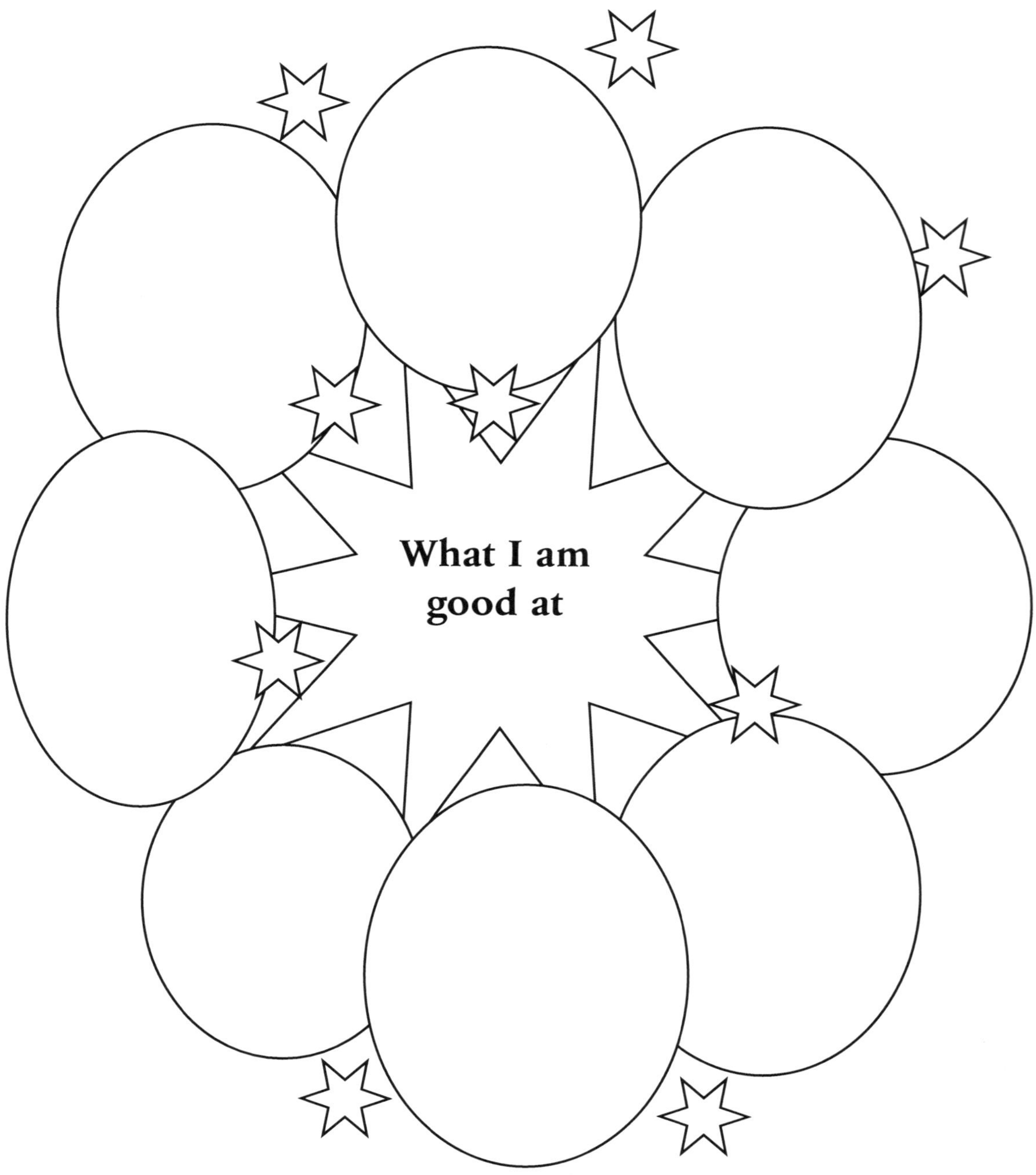

WORKSHEET 7: AFFIRMATIONS (2)

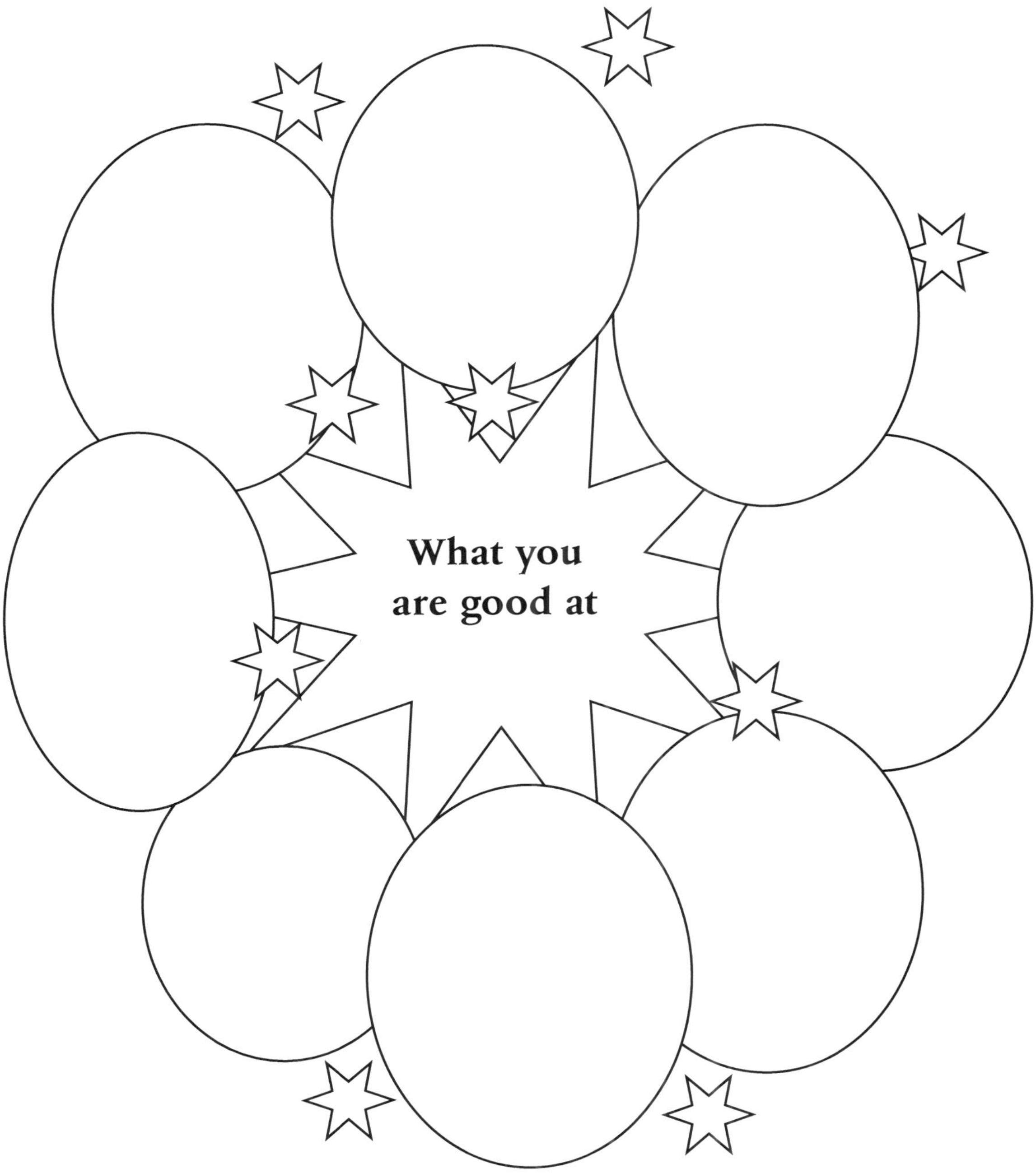

WORKSHEET 7: AFFIRMATIONS (3)

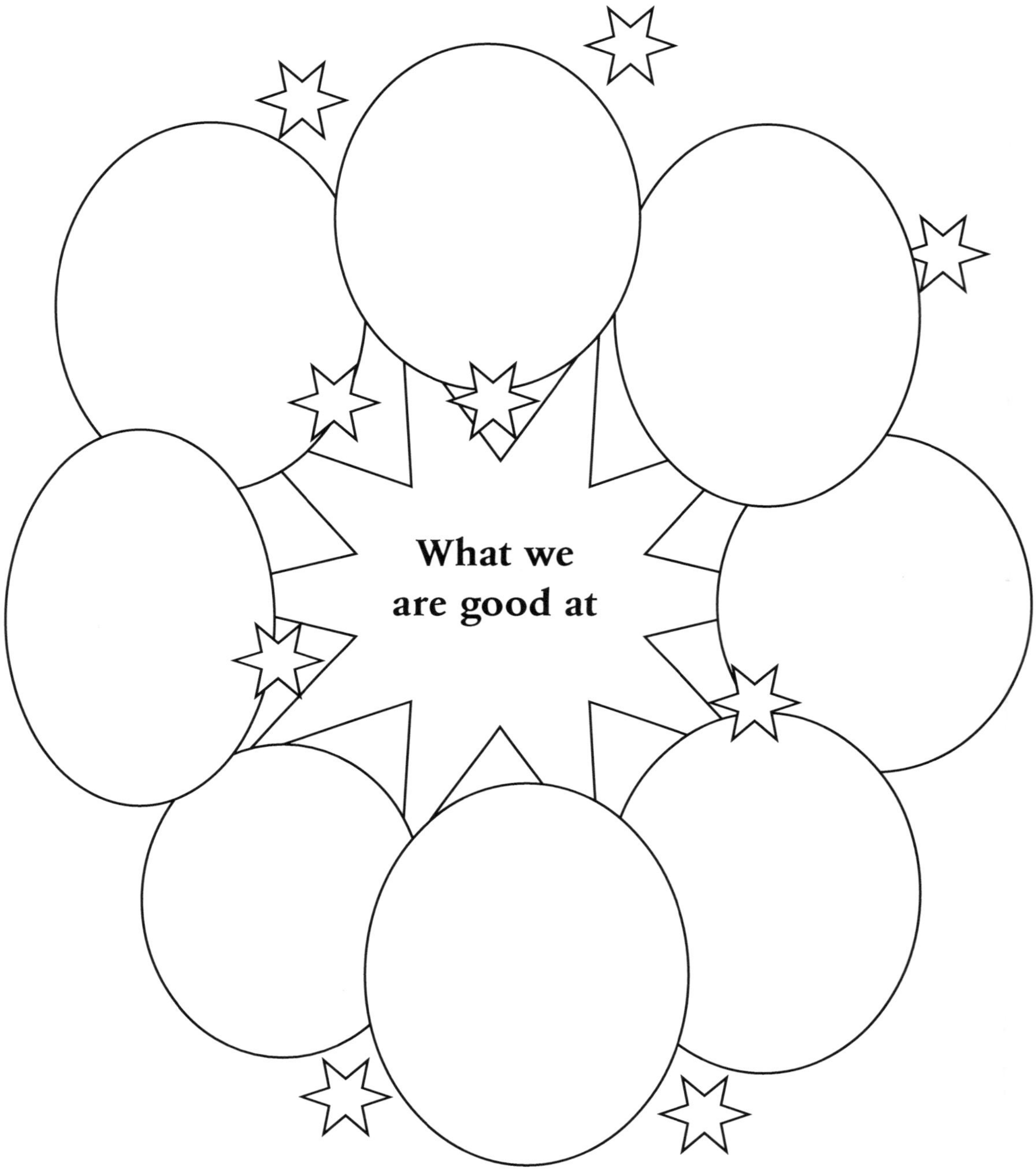

WORKSHEET 8: THOUGHTS AND FEELINGS

What we think and how we feel make up a large part of who we are. Jot down some answers to the following questions.

What *thoughts* make you feel good? ☺

1.
2.
3.

What *thoughts* make you feel bad? ☹

1.
2.
3.

What *feelings* do you like? ☺

1.
2.
3.

What *feelings* do you dislike? ☹

1.
2.
3.

✓

WORKSHEET 9: WHAT ARE YOUR PREFERRED SENSES?

Most of us have a preferred or dominant learning sense through which we take in information. The following chart helps you discover if your preferred sense is visual (V), aural (A) or kinaesthetic (physical) (K), or a combination of these.

Choose *one* of the following answers for each question (by circling V, A or K), and tally your results. The sense with the highest tally is your preferred sense.

Questions: When you...	**Answers:** Do you...	
spell a word	* 'picture' it in your mind so that it 'looks' right?	V
	* pronounce it out aloud, so that it 'sounds' right?	A
	* write it down so that it 'feels' right?	K
are concentrating	* become distracted by any surrounding untidiness?	V
	* become distracted by noises?	A
	* become distracted by movement around you?	K
praise or reward someone	* prefer to write them a congratulatory note?	V
	* tend to give them mostly verbal praise?	A
	* prefer to give them a handshake or pat on the back?	K
meet someone for the first time	* afterwards remember how they looked?	V
	* remember mostly what was said at the time?	A
	* remember what happened and how you felt?	K
see a movie or read a novel	* remember best what the scenes looked like?	V
	* remember best what was said, and the music?	A
	* remember best what happened, and the emotions?	K
assemble new equipment	* first read the instructions?	V
	* first read instructions aloud, and maybe ask for help?	A
	* first work with the pieces and try to put it together?	K
interact with other people	* prefer to draw or doodle or look about?	V
	* prefer to talk to them?	A
	* prefer to walk about, getting a 'feeling' for them?	K
memorize something	* write down what you are trying to remember?	V
	* repeat aloud what you are trying to remember?	A
	* pace up and down until you feel you've 'got it'?	K
talk	* talk quite fast, but always try to stay on the point?	V
	* talk fluently and clearly and at a fairly even pace?	A
	* speak with energy and expressive movements?	K
are angry	* become silent, keeping your feelings to yourself?	V
	* express yourself in verbal outbursts?	A
	* storm about, shaking your fists or throwing things?	K

